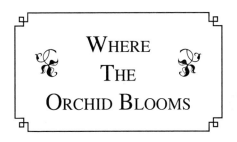

WHERE THE ORCHID BLOOMS

Written by D. Levy

One Family's Successful Journey Through Autism

Cover Photographer: Craig Levy
Graphic Designer: Linda Towner

ISBN 978-0-9966757-2-7

Printed by Industrial Printers of Colorado Inc.
110 E Enterprise
Colorado Springs, Co. 80918

Printed in the United States of America

For more information, or to order this book, please contact:
DLevywheretheorchidblooms@yahoo.com

WHERE THE ORCHID BLOOMS

This is the humorous, heartwarming story
of Kyle Levy and his successful journey
through Autism, as well as amputation,
after returning to the United States from Thailand.
He accomplished his dreams, despite discrimination,
through courage, faith and hope.
Kyle achieved his goal of becoming
an Air Plane Mechanic/Inspector,
using his prosthetic arm,
with laughter and determination.
He has won several awards for helping others,
and now inspires people
struggling with similar challenges.
This is the true story of Kyle's celebration of life.

I dedicate this book to Amanda and Susan.
    Amanda inspired Kyle
    And Susan inspired me to write this story.

ACKNOWLEGEMENTS

The people mentioned in this book graciously consented to allow their names to be used.

All other names have been changed to protect the privacy of the individuals and are noted by quotation marks.

I would like to thank Ranger Amanda for her generosity of spirit and complete acceptance of Kyle. This kindness profoundly changed Kyle's life.

Thank you to Ron for giving Kyle the example of hard work and a job well done.

I want to extend my profound thanks to Jeanne, Dave and Jaime. Kyle is a success today because of your willingness to take a chance and give him his first job in Aviation.

I would also like to thank Dr. Wilkins for his humorous encouragement. This support inspired Kyle to look beyond his challenges to succeed. We will always be grateful.

A special thanks to Ruth whose optimism and strength guided Kyle in his darkest moments.

Coach, wherever you are, your leadership and example allowed Kyle to follow his dreams with conviction. God Bless You always.

This book wouldn't have been written without the love and spirit-filled enthusiasm from my cousin Susan. Thank you for lifting me up in prayer during this journey.

Thank you Tina for being my friend and lifting me up with laughter during my darkest moments.

Thank you to my daughter Cat who was my editor, think tank, reality check and advisor. You made this book possible.

Thank you, finally, to my husband Rick who walked this journey with me and never gave up on our son. There are no words of thanks sufficient for your commitment and sacrifice.

TABLE OF CONTENTS

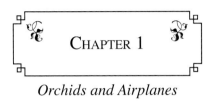

CHAPTER 1

Orchids and Airplanes

Orchids grow upside down hanging from trees in the shade. They thrive in the rain, not the sun, and out of an intangible twisted mass a magnificent flower blooms. The fragrance fills the air beyond the moss and shadows to delight anyone who comes across one in the Jungle. My son, Kyle, has always loved Orchids.

I think my son has always identified with the Orchid in the Jungle. Kyle is Autistic. We didn't know he had Autism until it was almost too late. This is his story.

My son was born in The Pacific Northwest of the United States of America. He was born at 10:10 in the morning on a summer day, which I always thought auspicious, since the number One is the beginning of all journeys.

I had no idea.

Kyle was a loveable looking Charlie Brown character. His head seemed impossibly big for his little body. He was born with no hair and his eyes were wide open. The Nurse midwife, who helped deliver him, remarked that she had never seen a baby born with his eyes open in all her years delivering babies.

I thought that was auspicious too.

We brought him home to two excited dogs. The Akita,

Sake, sat down next to him and curiously cocked one eye-brow. He took one sniff and sneezed. Our Scottish terrier, Whiskey, jumped up to get a good look at him. Whiskey promptly began rooting around his diaper and then looked at me quizzically as if to say, "What is this funny smelling creature?" But our cat, Scrimshaw who was a white Turkish Angora with a curious meow that sounded like she was demon possessed, curled up beside him and fell asleep.

It was love at first sight. Kyle adored Scrimshaw. I had to make sure the cat didn't give Kyle a daily tongue bath. The cat was quiet, and that fascinated Kyle. His eyes would follow her wherever she went.

My husband, Rick, was a Marine fighter pilot during his tour of duty. He proudly took Kyle to all the Air shows from the moment he was born. The air shows were performed at an Air Force base located just outside of Spokane, Washington. The air shows were open to the public for Armed Forces day and our family never missed one. We would take turns wheeling Kyle around in his baby stroller to look at all the aircraft on display. Kyle would race around the larger aircraft when he grew older. Rick would sometimes take him into these larger "birds" and seat him in the cockpits. It wasn't long before he could tell the difference and iden-tify the planes. Rick would hold him up and show him the Air force Thunderbirds or the Navy Blue Angels. Rick had been scheduled for Top Gun as a Marine pilot. He especially loved to put Kyle on the wings of the F-4's which Rick used to fly. Kyle was looking out of the canopies of fighter jets before he could walk, with Rick whispering in his ear that someday he would fly planes. Sometimes I would feel nervous as I watched him walk on the wings while holding on to his father.

All new mothers are nervous, and I was no exception. I labored over seemingly silly things: Am I using too much ointment or not enough, is he warm or too cold? I was fascinated by this tiny creation that seemed to change on a daily basis.

The first thing I remember was his smile. He smiled when I said his name. He seemed in awe of everything around him. He especially loved being rocked or being in motion of any kind.

I took him everywhere. I read to him from the beginning. We played learning games. His favorite books rhymed or were about mechanical things: trains, trucks and machines. We read these daily to the point where I recited them from memory. I created some of my own rhyme games. I would say, "This is your toe, this is your nose. This is a tree, this is your knee." I played endless rhyming games with him. He would laugh and point to anything he wanted me to name.

We also went to the park every morning. We would play the name game and then he would swing on the swings. Sometimes he would navigate the jungle gyms. I put him on the slide and held his hand until he safely landed on his feet by himself. We went every morning, no matter the weather, to explore the park. Kyle delighted in watching the birds or the squirrels. He would chase after them and watch the birds fly into the trees. He especially loved rainy days and would look up into the sky to let the rain fall on his cheeks. He would hold out his tiny hands to catch the rain, only to look at me and wonder where the rain drops went as they slid down onto the grass.

I let him watch videos on the Alphabet, Numbers or

"The Little Toaster" while I was cooking every afternoon. One day after watching machines in search of energy, Kyle decided that our video player was hungry too. I looked up just as he tried to feed it a peanut butter sandwich.

"No!" I shouted as I raced downstairs. I picked him up and grabbed the sandwich out of his hands.

"Mommy, it's hungry." He said as he patted me knowingly.

"Honey, the video player has its own food and he's already full," I assured him.

I hugged him close with eyes wide with relief.

He believed that machines were living things. His favorite toy was a train that ran around the Christmas tree.

I labored over teaching him his first word which I assumed would be "Mommy." After all…we were buddies playing all day together, right?

"Mommy, say Mommy," I would say all day long.

Eventually, my husband came home.

"Daddy," Kyle shouted!

Daddy was Kyle's first word. My mouth dropped to the floor. I shouted "Do over," and tried to make him take it back while my husband grabbed Kyle and said, "Hey Bud, nice going." Rick arched his eyebrow and smiled triumphantly, and so it was that I recorded his first words. Of course, I was grumbling under my breath…."Daddy".

This was followed by "No," and then the long awaited, "Ma."

I noticed Kyle would pat me when saying "Ma." He would fold his fingers toward himself if he wanted something and push on anything he didn't. This resulted, one day, in a plate full of peas pushed to the floor followed by two excited dogs chasing them all over the kitchen, while dragging Kyle along in his high chair. I was in a panic trying to stop the high chair and yelled at the dogs, "NO, NO, NO." Finally, I threw my hands up in the air, resigned to let them have the peas. Sake looked up at me with his muzzle now green, and I gave him a menacing look, "I hope you puke." I regretted saying that later realizing that I would have to clean THAT up too.

Kyle never crawled, he climbed. He climbed up on top of the refrigerator while I searched everywhere for him in a panic. It never occurred to me to look UP until the cat meowed and started pawing up at Kyle from the counter.

He smiled and reached for me with a happy grin. After all, what was all the fuss about? When he couldn't climb, he reached up to grasp anything to help him stand, and soon he was running. Kyle ran on his toes and loved to run in place especially when watching movies about runners. I enjoyed watching him pretend to be the fastest runner on the planet when he raced around the house. I was surprised by his growl whenever he ran or concentrated on a serious task. The most serious task for Kyle was the stairs.

Kyle was fascinated by stairs and practiced all day until he mastered them. He never gave up. I was terrified when he was determined to do the same on the jungle gym in the park. He was happy as long as he was moving.

Sometimes, the only way to get Kyle to sleep was by putting him in the car where he would close his eyes to the rhythm of the ride. So, I would buy a cup of coffee and take long drives in the country listening to Mahalia Jackson, Shirley Cesar or the Staple Singers gospel. Sometimes we would listen to Blue Grass. Somehow, when Kyle had colic, it calmed me down too. The days passed like a wonderful dream despite the colic until one day, he just wouldn't stop crying.

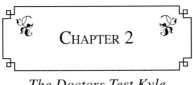

CHAPTER 2

The Doctors Test Kyle

I knew what to do for the colic, realizing that I was burping Kyle the wrong way. I had it down to a science and felt tremendous relief when I heard these huge belches from such a tiny child. He had a fever and rubbed his eyes so I called and made a doctors appointment.

The doctors said he had an ear infection. Oh, and it was time for his two year vaccinations.

He stopped crying but seemed listless and lethargic.

I took him for a check up and he still had the infection, so they changed the antibiotic for another round.

By the third round they eyed me suspiciously.

"What kind of environment is he in?" one doctor asked me.

"We just moved into a new house," I mumbled surprised.

"Oh, well there may be chalk dust and particulate matter in the air," he replied while writing on his note pad. He turned to me with an after thought and raised his eyebrow suspiciously.

"Do you smoke?" he asked critically.

"Yes, but only at night and never around the baby." I replied.

"How much do you smoke?" he said now fully glaring.

"Does that matter? I don't smoke around Kyle....I smoke 3 cigarettes a day, at night after he goes to bed," I countered defensively.

I felt like a felon. Naturally if the doctors couldn't find out what was wrong with him, then I MUST BE DOING SOMETHING WRONG.

It was nonsense, and I knew it but somehow the authority of the Almighty Stethoscope made me pause uncertainly. I looked at my son's beautiful face and determined to stop smoking. I went to counseling several weeks later in an effort to quit.

I became pregnant again soon after I started counseling, and morning sickness became the answer to my prayers. I stopped smoking completely. Kyle continued to have chronic ear infections.

The doctors suggested we put tubes in his ears. I questioned them on the success rate of this procedure. The success rate couldn't be guaranteed or that he would have fewer ear infections. It seemed obvious to me that tubes and cotton swabbing in the ears would make him more prone to infections, not less prone.

This time I was strong in my stance: No tubes.

He eventually stopped having ear infections.

My daughter was born during this time. When I brought her home from the hospital, he took one look at her and said, "Mine." He had the sweetest smile on his face. I got a chill when he said it. It was as if he was saying she was born just for me, and I believed him.

It was during this time that I noticed Kyle wasn't talking the way other babies did at his age.

I took him back to the doctor.

"I know I'm just a first time mom, but shouldn't he be talking at two and a half years old?" I asked unsure of myself.

The doctor watched us for several minutes and said, "Well, you know what he wants without a word." The doctor chuckled. "You're going to have to make him talk by making him ask for what he needs. This is not unusual. Some kids are either verbal or tactile. I bet he's a real active boy." I nodded. He was constantly challenging himself on the older kids' jungle gyms at the park, endlessly trying to master his physical world.

Thus began the battle of words. Kyle knew that I knew what he wanted by a hand gesture. When I insisted that he use a word to describe what he wanted, we struggled. He would become enraged. He would scream at the top of his lungs and throw himself on the floor to kick at anything close. One time, Kyle threw cereal at me in absolute disgust. And sometimes, he would hide his face in my shoulder as if talking took so much effort that he sadly couldn't bear it. At those times, I would hold him gently and explain to him that he had to learn to talk with his mouth and not his hands. There were moments when we both cried. It was if he knew he had to do it, but became exhausted by the effort and I knew I had to push him with a grim sadness that was hard to bear for me.

Eventually, I noticed that Kyle had no concept of the word "I". I would insist that "You" wanted an apple and he would equally insist that Kyle wanted an apple...not I, me or you. He referred to everything as "Kyle wants, Kyle goes, Mommy wants, Daddy goes." I would repeat that "I" wanted an apple while touching his chest and then put his hand on my chest to say "you" want an apple. "You" was the third person in the room and not "Mommy". I saw the logic of his thinking and sympathized but I repeated this exercise daily hoping that by repetition, he would eventually absorb the concept of "Me" and "You".

By the time he was three, he was still speaking in two word sentences. I found if I used more than two words to communicate with him he became confused. He would stop in mid stride and look at me quizzically. It was as if he was trying to figure out the priority of the words. If I said, "Go to the door and get the dog", he would shake his head and sometimes go to the dog, or go to the door. He couldn't put them together in the sequence I said the words. Kyle would rub his eyes or stop in confusion and just stand there trying to figure out what I said. But that was no indication of his intelligence. He knew all his colors, he knew his numbers to 10, and A-Z.

I also noticed other things, small things at first. He lined his toys up every night in a straight line against the wall. His shoes were in a perfect straight line in his closet and he would get agitated if you rearranged them.

I arranged for a play date with a little girl who lived down the street. She was a playful child and when she noticed his toys all in a row, she began to throw them up in the air. My son became enraged and began shouting.

"No Dat, NO DAT!" Kyle growled.

Then he put all the toys back in the exact order. I shook my head and decided it was snack time which ended this little drama.

He also dragged a bunny around all day long with his Blue Peter Rabbit blanket. He thought the bunny was alive. I washed the stuffed animal one day while he was taking a nap. He awoke and ran downstairs looking for Bunny. When he realized that the rabbit was in the washing machine, he screamed, "You killed bunny. YOU KILLED BUNNY!" I was thrilled he had gotten the concept of you, and horrified that he was glaring at me with absolute prejudice.

I had to assure him that bunny was just getting a bath. I opened the washing machine and showed him an extremely soggy bunny. I realized immediately that I had to tell Kyle the washing machine was just for Bunny and not a place for Kyle to take a bath. Horrible images ran through my mind of Kyle dangerously trying to bathe with Bunny. (I had to wash bunny late at night from that day on.) He really seemed to think inanimate objects were alive. He would pat the vacuum cleaner and talk to the toaster. He would carry his lamp as a friend which I'm sure resulted from his love of the movie about a toaster in search of energy. I chalked this up to childhood fantasy and smiled at his "friends."

I also noticed routine was very important. If I didn't prepare Kyle for any deviation in our routine, he would become extremely agitated. He also could only handle places like the mall or grocery store for 1 hour. After that he would become over stimulated and "zone" out or become uncontrollable. When he became over stimulated, he would stop and look around him in a daze. Sometimes, Kyle would just stop and stare up at the ceiling. If I changed our routine, he would growl or throw himself on the ground and engage in a full scale tantrum. I would look at him in horror when he did this. I felt that this was more than just being cranky, tired and overwhelmed. If I prepared him for the changes and kept our activities sequential with a lot of advanced preparation, then he could transition. I was continually describing his world and the part we would play in it, but it seemed extreme at times to me.

I took him back to the doctor.

The doctors suggested I take him to the local University to have him tested.

He was tested.

The young female intern came out to speak with me. She seemed sweet and terrified.

"Mrs. Levi...." She mumbled in a high breathy voice.

"It's Levy," I countered smiling.

"Mrs. Levi...we're going to be doing some exercises today with bunnies and eggs and um...ugh..." she stammered.

I looked around at all the Easter decorations with sudden understanding.

"And you want to know if I'm Jewish?" I laughed. "I don't have the privilege of being Jewish. God had a sense of humor and put me in an Irish Catholic family....so Easter egg away. "

She laughed nervously, visibly relieved.

The young intern eventually determined that Kyle had AUDITORY PROCESSING DISORDER.

It was explained to me. I said, "Kyle, go to the door." And he heard, "Kyle door go to the." She explained that he had to work harder than most kids his age to understand what I meant despite what he heard.

No wonder he hesitated and seemed confused at times.

We began working with a speech therapist twice a week through the summer and Kyle seemed to be progressing. I used to let Kyle pick music for car rides during that time. He always chose the same songs for different places to go: Christmas songs for the store, Heavy Metal for Speech Therapy and Alvin and the Chipmunk songs for school.

We also were potty training to prepare Kyle for preschool.

I made the mistake of letting him stand during this process only to have to "spring clean" the bathroom ceiling several minutes later. (I never had brothers and had NO IDEA.) I insisted he sit during potty exercises. He "worked" for chocolate M&M's, so it was going fairly well until my husband came home one day. He insisted that a real MAN stands.

"Its okay honey, some things a MAN has to show another MAN," Rick smiled knowingly.

I sighed and nodded skeptically.

He marched Kyle upstairs. "Come on Bud, I'll show you how it's done," he said confidently.

I was chopping vegetables for dinner. I stopped to listen.

"Hey, Buddy…that's great," Rick said

"Really, Daddy?" said Kyle turning to look at Rick.

"Yeah, Buddy, that's great…Goddamn it, Jesus Christ!" yelled Rick. "Look where you're pointing that thing."

Yep. I knew it.

A few minutes later Rick came walking downstairs. He had changed his pants.

"Don't say it, just don't say it," he grumbled.

I started to laugh silently and couldn't stop until I was laughing so loud that tears were streaming down my face. I watched him put his pants in the washing machine while shaking his head.

"Sitting down?" I said as I poured him a glass of wine.

"Yeah, he sits down for now," he nodded.

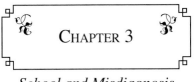

CHAPTER 3

School and Misdiagnosis

Kyle turned four that summer and we began looking for preschools.

I enrolled him in the most expensive and elite preschool. I was thinking that I was such a great Mom to give him this opportunity despite the cost.

He lasted one day.

The teacher told me not to bring him back. He was "a disruption" to the class.

"What kind of a disruption?" I asked horrified.

"He won't sit still." She sniffed.

"He's a boy, he's just turned four...they don't sit still at four!" I countered incredulously.

"He's a disruption, thank you for coming." She said arching her eyebrow and sniffing into her hand.

And just like that we were dismissed.

Peering into the classroom window, I looked at the other students. They all seemed dull and cowed compared to Kyle's energy and enthusiasm.

I went to another preschool and then another and another. I went to one school during a lunch hour and spoke to the secretary about returning when the principal finished her lunch.

"The principal will be back at a quarter to one," she shrugged while chewing the most enormous piece of gum I've ever seen.

"Okay," I smiled, "I'll be back at 12:45".

"No," she said with a huff while glaring at me menacingly. "A Quarter TO ONE."

I tried unsuccessfully to contain my laughter but only made it to the door. You know, those giggles you get in church...the harder you hold it in...the more you laugh until its uncontrollable.

I laughed all the way home.

And then I cried.

I told my husband later that night that I was starting to despair of ever finding a good preschool. Any principal who hired a receptionist that stupid and bad mannered had no business teaching ANYONE.

Still, how does one get rejected from PRESCHOOL?

"Isn't that where kids learn social skills like sitting still?" I asked Rick. "He already knows the kindergarten curriculum–I taught him that over the summer," I muttered.

"I don't know, Honey," my husband replied worriedly.

We sat there for a few minutes in silence. He suggested the last school on the list. It was the Catholic school.

"But you're not Catholic, you're Protestant," I said surprised.

He shrugged. "It's just pre-school."

I nodded and chewed my lip nervously. I remembered all the stories my mother told me from her childhood during the 40's: Nuns with rulers that served as modern day torture devices leaving rapped knuckles bruised or bleeding; Paddles that had holes drilled into them so the priest could whack you

26

harder if you skipped to Mass or whistled near the altar. "Just Preschool?" I thought. "Dear Mary mother of God," I muttered to myself the next day as I drove up to the Catholic preschool to meet the teacher. "I must be insane."

Standing there at the top of the driveway was a tall, friendly woman named "Miss C". She had a no nonsense attitude and a smile from ear to ear.

I liked her immediately.

She said she would accept Kyle after hearing my story. She would watch him for a few days and give me an assessment.

I got a call that night.

Kyle was uncontrollable when I left and Miss C had to use the two armed "hug" to calm him down several times. She said that he became inconsolable during any transition from activity to activity. If he was approached by the other children, he would growl at them like a dog while curling his little fists. If someone spoke to him or directed him to do something suddenly without repeating several times what was coming, he would throw himself on the ground kicking and screaming.

It occurred to me that, at home, I noticed transition was hard for Kyle. I just assumed it was his personality, so I gently repeated several times the steps we were about to take or the places we would go. Sometimes it seemed extreme, but taking the time to prepare him seemed kind and perfectly natural to me. I would automatically tell him that I was going to hug him; otherwise my sudden movement would frighten him. Any sudden noise would make him cry. He loved to play quietly, building things or taking things apart endlessly. He was fascinated by the toys that turned into other things and electrical appliances. These were things that moved and could be rearranged. Even if I warned him that I was about to vacuum, the sound made him cry.

So, one day, I made him vacuum to master his fear. It worked that day until the next time I had to vacuum. I found he learned by gentle, persistent, repetitive doing. Talking or reading left him dazed, but touch or holding and feeling the lessons became real to him. He did learn from the educational videos on T.V. and I would watch him; he was fascinated by the movement of the pictures. Movement was the key to Kyle's understanding; either he or his world had to be in movement.

The only time he was content to sit for long periods was when Rick took Kyle fishing. Our family would drive north to a Lake which was surrounded by National Forest in Stevens County. We would pack a picnic lunch and go up there for the day. Rick could get away from phones, stress and work that inevitably followed a Federal Agent home. Kyle was four when Rick first began teaching him to fish. The lake was stocked with Rainbow Trout and Kyle was fascinated as he watched his father thread a worm on the hook. Rick would cast the bait out into the lake, propped the pole on a stick and instructed Kyle to watch the fishing rod tip for "bites". He was mesmerized by the machinery of the fishing line and the sparkle on the water made by the sun. He would sit still and hyper focus on the anticipated fish. He was still only four years old and inevitably Kyle would begin to play with the worms, bugs or butterflies around the lake.

One day, Kyle was chasing a butterfly when Rick saw the rod tip of the fishing pole dancing, which indicated a fish was playing with the bait. He ran to the rod while calling for Kyle.

"Come quick," he yelled.

Rick got to the rod and set the hook as Kyle came running. It was obvious that they had a fish on the line. Rick gave him the fishing pole and instructed him to reel it in. He started reeling in the line. He hauled the fish to the surface where it started to splash. This startled Kyle. He tried to hand the rod back to Rick, but Rick was determined that Kyle was going to catch this fish. Rick gently pushed the rod back to Kyle and instructed him to keep the rod tip high.

"Keep reeling him in, Kyle–slowly. YOU CAN DO IT!" Rick whispered.

Kyle went back to working the reel. The fish was splashing and fighting as Kyle slowly pulled it to shore. Once the fish was on the shoreline, Kyle became really excited. Rick reached down and grabbed the fish bringing it up so Kyle could admire it. It was a beautiful Rainbow Trout that was about 12 inches long. Rick showed him how to gently hold the fish while removing the hook. Kyle put the fish on a stringer that was placed in the water to keep the fish fresh.

"That was a great job, Kyle! Congratulations!" Rick beamed.

Kyle ran to me and, grabbing my arm, dragged me to the fish. We all admired his handiwork and praised him.

"You'll be able to feed your family someday. I'm very proud of you," I whispered in his ear as I hugged him.

It was one of those moments that your mind captures like a snapshot, because on some level you know the moment was profound for everyone.

We brought the fish home that evening and Kyle watched intently as Rick cleaned it. He gave Kyle a biology lesson on fish explaining the various organs inside. Kyle wasn't squeamish at all.

"Would you like to see what the fish has been eating, Kyle?" laughed Rick.

Kyle nodded with excitement.

Rick cut open the stomach and spread the contents out to show mostly insects. Kyle followed this biology lesson seriously and from that time on he insisted on examining the stomach contents of every catch.

We prepared the fish and fried it up. We served it for dinner that night. Kyle was beaming about being the one who caught dinner for the family. He devoured the fish and we sensed that a "fisherman" was born. Kyle loved fishing from that moment on. He loved the quiet, peaceful surroundings and the excitement of the catch. Whenever Rick had a day off and could spend time with Kyle, Kyle always pleaded with him to go fishing up north.

Rick took Kyle shopping for his own fishing rod. Kyle picked out a child size rod and reel which he used for the next several years. Whenever we could get away from the pressures of Rick's work, we would go fishing or camping. We would hike, paddle boat and swim. We told ghost stories around the campfire with a flashlight under Ricks face and laughed as the children would scream with delight. They would run into the tent, only to peek out again to see if we were still there. Rick laughed that Kyle's fish were always bigger than the ones he caught. Kyle loved running and playing, especially in the woods. He was happiest when running.

I thought of all this after Miss C's initial assessment. Kyle was my first born so I had nothing with which to compare his behavior. I just assumed this to be normal for boys. After all, I had grown up with sisters. I just took it for granted that boys were more active.

I took it for granted until my daughter, Caitlin, began growing.

She was so much more verbal than Kyle, but just as active. She was always running after Kyle. She quickly grasped concepts in the abstract while Kyle was literal about everything. One day in the middle of dinner, for example, she made an intuitive leap.

She farted.

There was silence, and then she giggled embarrassed.

"Excuse me, I made a butt burp," she laughed.

"No, Keys," replied Kyle. "Butts don't burp. Only mouths burp."

"MY BUTT BURPED and don't call me Keys. My name is CAITLIN!" she yelled adamantly in indignation.

I laughed so hard, I almost fell off my chair.

Kyle and his father had an argument a few days later. Rick told Kyle to clean his room. Kyle replied, "Say peas." Rick growled back, "Just do it." Kyle curled his little fists, "IF I GOTTA SAY PEAS, YOU GOTTA SAY PEAS!" I yelled up to an exasperated Rick, "For God's sake, JUST SAY PEAS, PLEASE, you know what I mean."

Kyle took manners literally, just like language, and had a strong sense of equality.

Miss C called me in for a teacher conference several weeks later.

She couldn't understand Kyle and wanted him professionally assessed. She said he was 2 years ahead academically, but 2 years behind socially. He did not deal well with other children. The exception was his sister. He isolated himself repeatedly.

I nodded and made an appointment with a specialist.

The doctor assessed him and concluded that he was "probably ADHD," or Attention Deficit Hyperactivity Disorder with the possibility of mild retardation.

I stared blankly at the doctor. Mildly retarded? I felt shock and began to fume.

"Doctor, his teacher says he's 2 years ahead academically. That doesn't sound like mental retardation to me," I grumbled. "What causes ADHD?"

"We don't know," he replied. "Did you smoke while you were pregnant?"

"I stopped when I found out I was pregnant."

"Did you drink while you were pregnant?" he countered.

"Only the last month. My sister said that a cup of beer was prescribed by her Canadian doctor to produce milk in first time mothers," I replied.

He smirked knowingly at me, "I see."

"Are you saying I caused this? I thought you said the medical community doesn't know what causes ADHD?" I started to really get angry.

He shrugged, "That's true. We don't."

He suggested I put Kyle on medicine to help with the hyperactivity.

I shook my head. "I'm going to try and see if I can help him naturally without drugs."

The doctor was cynical. "You can try, but it's going to get harder and harder for him to sit still and pay attention."

I left disgusted and called my husband. I wanted a second opinion. The "mild retardation" assessment after only one hour seemed off the wall to me compared to Kyle's advanced knowledge in certain subjects.

Later that night I talked with Rick.

"They told my mom that I was retarded in Kindergarten after being tested one afternoon. My mom cried all the way home. A year later I was tested again and, all of a sudden, I was "gifted–a creative thinker". I was the same kid; different label. They can't possibly know any of this after 60 minutes."

"You were called retarded? You graduated first in your major in college." My husband was shocked.

"Yeah, I made up my own story about Chicken Little. I didn't like the idea of a sky falling, so I changed the story as quickly as I read it. By the time they realized that I could actually read it, they had to change the assessment."

My father, a tough former Detroit cop and Marine, called later that day. I told him the doctors thought Kyle was retarded. He was silent for a moment.

"They told Edison he was retarded too. Forget it, kid," my Dad said.

"Thanks, Dad," I whispered. It was the first good news I had heard all day.

And so, I began really watching Kyle through the next few weeks. He still had trouble with loud noises. Whenever the vacuum made him cry, Caitlin would walk over to the vacuum and kick it.

Rick was gone during these weeks on business, so we started having "picnics in the rain". We would put a blanket on the floor and put our favorite foods from the deli spread out like a picnic. We would watch scary movies like this every Saturday night. We would laugh and cuddle. Kyle would laugh at the monsters and throw popcorn at the screen.

He wasn't frightened at all by these silly creatures. Caitlin, on the other hand, would pull the covers up to her neck to keep the "Dracleas" or Vampires from biting her. Eventually, Rick had to trim back the tree branches that scratched against her window because she was convinced the "Dracleas" were scratching at her window trying to get in.

I also began keeping a food diary and watching Kyle's behavior after he ate certain foods. I charted these over several months until the spring. Miss C was very supportive of my efforts. She also encouraged me to keep Kyle in preschool a second year. She felt he just wasn't emotionally ready for Kindergarten. I agreed. It didn't seem too important at his age since he had just turned 4 the previous August. I continued the food diary through the summer and noticed a pattern emerge: FISH OIL VS. CARBOHYDRATES.

I found whenever Kyle had carbohydrates such as wheat, rice, potato, corn or oats, he became unfocused. Sugars made him hyperactive, but even non-sugared cereals made him glaze over dreamily. I found that any kind of fish, especially salmon, sardines and tuna, made him calm, hyper-focused and able to learn. He developed sensitivity to citric acid that summer which gave him a condition called "geographic tongue". These were crater like sores on his tongue that were painful for him, so, I tried to give him vitamin C with more broccoli and apples.

My daughter was weary of these "little trees." She refused to eat them one evening.

I looked at her and said there were starving children in the world who would love to eat the broccoli she had on her plate. She looked at me for a moment and thought about it.

"Here, Mommy. Let's give it to them!" she decided. No

amount of reasoning could convince her otherwise. There were other children more in need of her little trees.

September came too suddenly. Kyle started Preschool with Miss C for the second year. He did remarkably well. I had home schooled him over the summer to keep his skills up, since he spent most of his time learning to cope with social skills in class.

He was very popular with the little girls. He came home and told us that he had a "date" with a girl named "J". Kyle asked if I could drive them to the movies.

"Isn't it cute?" I laughed to my husband.

"He's a little young, isn't he?" Rick countered while rolling his eyes.

"I don't know," I laughed. "I seem to recall getting a Batman ring from a boy when I was his age."

Kyle did so well Miss C recommended that he go on to kindergarten.

That summer I continued to watch Kyle. We went to the playground almost every day.

One day we went to the playground and, after a few minutes, a woman approached me.

"Is that your son?" she asked. She seemed upset.

"Yes," I replied tentatively.

"Your son just called me fat."

I called Kyle over to us and asked him to apologize.

He refused.

"Kyle, you will apologize to this woman right now or we're going home and you'll be given a time out." I was speaking more loudly now.

Kyle refused.

I apologized for my son's rudeness and then grabbed

Kyle by the arm.

"Let's go!" I said gritting my teeth.

I marched him and Caitlin to the car. I sat there a few moments and looked at my son.

"Kyle, why wouldn't you apologize?" I asked shaking my head.

"Because it was true, Mom. She WAS fat."

"Kyle, just because something is true, that doesn't mean it's always kind to say it. She may be fat, or fat to YOU, but someone else may not find her fat."

"She WAS fat," Kyle stated with the defiance of a truth zealot.

"Kyle, I want you to listen to me very carefully. What you said was unkind and, worse, it was impolite. We have manners in this family and you are not allowed to say anything you like if it hurts other people. Do you understand? I mean it. I'm very disappointed in you and you will be punished if you do this again. Right now, you're going to have a time out before dinner."

I avoided that playground the rest of the summer and we started exploring other playgrounds.

I decided that Kyle and Caitlin were old enough to begin earning some of their own money. Everyday, I would have Kyle clean the toilet and Caitlin would clean the sink. I would make a big ceremony of giving them each a quarter when they were finished, which they would deposit in a giant plastic crayon bank. We would go "garage sailing" at the end of the week. We would hop in the car with the dogs and explore different areas looking for the best sale. The kids would jump out. They would find some things and ask if I thought they had enough money to purchase them. It was a great way to teach them the value of work, counting, and what their money could buy. We would come home with our treasures: books, games, dolls and toys. Kyle would take the toys apart eventually to see how they worked. Caitlin, whom we now called Cat, would have me read the books over and over again. These were some of my most precious memories; those long summer days of exploration and play.

Kyle turned 6 that summer and we made a great treasure hunt for his birthday. I hid clues all over the house that eventually led to the backyard where the treasure was buried. Our backyard was designed for little children. We had several maple trees that turned different shades of red, orange and yellow. We had also planted plum trees, a cherry tree and lots of lilac bushes. The trees and bushes made several hidden play areas that we had placed with mock castles and tents.

Kyle had found the last clue and dug up his treasure. It was a wooden box that I had spray painted gold and glued faux jewels on top. When he opened the box, he found gold coins that were filled with chocolate. He thought that was the greatest thing in the world. He carried that box and placed it next to his bed. He looked at that box every night and smiled.

A few weeks later, he found a dead bird in the backyard where the treasure chest had been. It was a baby sparrow. Kyle was very upset because it had no eyes and he started to cry. I explained that it had no eyes because it had died. The bird's soul was in heaven with God.

"Will God gave him eyes?" Kyle asked wiping his eyes with his arm

"Yes, I think God gave him beautiful eyes." I wondered at

this sensitivity that Kyle felt.

"Wait, Mom. Let's bury him," Kyle insisted excitedly.

We found an old small box and put a small washcloth in it so the bird would be warm. We buried it where Kyle's treasure was found and we said a prayer.

"Pease, God. Let this bird fly," Kyle whispered.

"Amen," I said wistfully.

Caitlin put a little daisy on his grave and I gave her a hug. The day was getting cold and it looked like a storm was coming.

"I think the rain is coming, Kyle." I pointed to the sky. "Look Cat, see the Thunder clouds?"

"Hooray! Let's have a picnic in the rain, Mom," Kyle and Caitlin both shouted.

"Okay," I agreed.

So we drove to the store and picked some fun foods that had to be healthy from the deli. As we were leaving, Cat noticed a Chocolate birthday cake and pointed to it.

"Let's get it, Mom!" she asked hopefully.

"Oh, Caitlin this is a birthday cake," I frowned.

"But it's my UN-birthday!" she giggled. I realized she had been watching "Alice in Wonderland".

I stood there stunned. I was so impressed with her logic that I went ahead and bought the cake.

"What are we celebrating?" my husband asked as he walked through the door after work.

"We're celebrating Cat's UN-birthday and a funeral," I laughed as I handed him a glass of wine. "I'll explain later."

Rick was able to join us for a picnic in the rain and we all cuddled on the blanket late into the night until the kids fell asleep.

The next day, Rick replaced the runners on Kyle's closet door. He made a great show of using the screwdriver to take out the screws and replace them. He let Kyle help him by turning the screws and then ceremoniously replaced the closet doors. I watched from the door and clapped when they were finished.

Kyle began taking the screw driver and taking things apart. It became his new favorite toy. I had to make him promise me that he would stop taking my kitchen appliances apart. I found him doing just that while walking upstairs one day from the basement. The electric can opener still worked, but it made a weird humming sound and I was afraid to use it. I decided to hide all the screwdrivers. I was convinced he was going to hurt himself and one day an appliance would explode.

I missed one.

I was reading one day after I put Kyle and Caitlin down for a nap.

BOOOM !

I went running upstairs and flew open the bedroom door.

Kyle had found one screwdriver and had inserted it into an electrical socket after having pried off the child safety plug. The only thing that saved him was he had put his rubber sneakers on. His hand was charred black and his shoe was on the other side of the room.

We had our first long talk about Electricity.

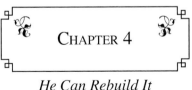

CHAPTER 4

He Can Rebuild It

The next day, Rick woke up and said he didn't feel well. He seemed pale and shaky. He said he felt weak and nauseous. I called the doctor and asked if he would see Rick. There had been a cancellation, so we packed up the kids and drove into town.

Kyle and Caitlin were playing in the doctor's waiting room. The doctor came out and kneeled in front of me. He quietly told me that Rick was having a heart attack. He put his hand on mine and said they were admitting him to the hospital.

Just at that moment, Kyle kicked the doctor.

"Kyle!" I shouted. "That was very rude. You will apologize, this instant."

The doctor just laughed nervously while Kyle apologized.

We drove to the hospital behind the ambulance. I held both the children's hands as I navigated the hospital corridors. I finally found the emergency room. We waited for what seemed like hours.

The doctor came out and told me that Rick could have a heart catheter, which would put a "stint" in one of the vessels of his heart to clear the blockage, or they could do a by pass. What did I want to do?

"Well, what does Rick want to do? I think he would

want the less invasive procedure, but I want you to ask him," I said.

"Oh, you don't understand. He's heavily sedated. He wouldn't be able to respond," the doctor countered with hesitation.

"You don't understand, Doctor. He's a Marine and a Federal Agent. He's had the same training under stress that you've had–I promise you he'll tell you what he wants."

The doctors came back several minutes later and they were dumbfounded.

"You were right. We asked him and he answered that he wants the stint."

"Okay, let's do the stint," I said softly in a daze.

Rick was taken to his room several hours later. The kids were restless and hungry, so I decided to take them home and return later. I was holding back the tears, exhausted, when I realized I was completely lost. We got onto an elevator and an elderly African American woman joined us. When we got to our floor, Kyle started towards the door. I held him back without thinking.

I said quietly, "No, no, Kyle. Elders first."

Caitlin yelled, "Yeah, Kyle, OLDERS FIRST." She was scowling at him.

I started to laugh as tears poured down my cheeks.

The woman stopped and smiled at me with surprised gratitude. Then as an afterthought, she asked me if I was lost. I nodded and she told me which direction I should take to find my car. I thanked her and we finally found our car. I drove home in a fog. I made the kids a late dinner of Mac and Cheese. I had just put them down to bed when I heard a loud thump coming from Kyle's room. I quietly walked upstairs and slowly opened the door. There was Kyle. He had taken the closet doors off the runners and was unscrewing them. I got a sense that in his mind if he undid the doors, he could undo the day. I knelt down and we talked about his father.

"Daddy's broke–the hos fu ful fix daddy?" Kyle asked.

I nodded and gave him a hug. We put the doors back in place. I tucked Kyle into bed and made him promise not to "fix" the doors anymore that night.

We went back to the hospital the next day. When Caitlin saw Rick in bed with all the tubes sticking out of him, she started to cry. Kyle tried to climb into the bed with Rick. He was fascinated by all the tubes and wires. I had come prepared. We had coloring books and crayons, treats and juice boxes. It was shift change and Rick said weakly that he didn't feel right.

I looked at the blood pressure machine and it read 60/40 and dropping. He broke out in a cold sweat and began to convulse. I started screaming for a nurse. One came and administered something. She apologized. She said he was going into shock for the second time that day. He went into shock during surgery because the initial stint had failed.

The doctor came and I mentioned that I thought Rick might be opiate sensitive.

"Is there anything else we can give him that will keep his vessels dilated that wasn't opiate based?" I asked.

"What do you mean, opiate sensitive?" he sneered.

At that moment, my blood boiled.

"I'll tell you what I mean, Doctor. I mean he broke out into a profuse sweat, his BP was 60 over 40 and dropping, he broke into convulsions. Opiates don't usually have that effect, do they Doctor? He should have had a slight tingling over his face, spreading warmth and feeling of euphoria! Now, WHAT CAN WE GIVE HIM?"

The doctor stopped. He asked if I would excuse him for a moment.

I heard him go into the hallway and ask one of the nurses, "Who IS she?"

"Oh," the nurse replied. "He's a Federal Agent and she used to be one too.

He returned a few seconds later and explained that the "nurses" had allowed Rick to become dehydrated. Rick wasn't sensitive at all. It wouldn't happen again and he apologized.

The nurse came into the room and smiled shyly.

"He's never apologized to anyone before. He's a real jerk." She whispered a nervous laugh and then cleared her throat.

I nodded and bit my lip. I felt like a terrier with a bone and from that moment I refused to leave Rick's side.

I found a babysitter to watch the kids and called Rick's mother to come. She flew out the next day and I picked her up from the airport. I explained that I wanted her to tell him he would be all right so that he would really believe it. He was having a hard time recovering after the two surgeries and the drugs. I was afraid for him

I was right. The minute Rick heard his mother say, "You're doing fine," he began to recover.

A few hours later, the nurses prepared us for the catheter removal from the femoral artery. They had just begun to pull the catheter out and put sand bags on Rick thigh when a window washer swung down in front of the window like Spider Man. He waved an embarrassed "Sorry" as his feet hit the glass. Rick began to laugh despite his horror at being completely "displayed" in front of this man washing the windows. We all howled.

Rick, thankfully, recovered and we brought him home the next day. It was several weeks before he felt himself again. Kyle asked him, "Where did all your wires go, Daddy?" Kyle expected to see them under his shirt.

Rick laughed, "I don't need wires anymore."

CHAPTER 5

The Prejudice of Kindergarten

Kyle started Kindergarten that fall and Caitlin started preschool. Kyle kicked and screamed to stay home just like the two years before. Caitlin barely waved goodbye when she started school with her brother. She was so excited to be with her big brother. I would work on her hair in the mornings, making pretty braids and ponytails with beautiful ribbons. When I dropped them off, I would see Caitlin pulling the ribbons from her hair. She would casually drop them on the floor. I would pick them up and pocket them with a sigh. Kyle was meticulous about his shoes, while Caitlin liked to put them on the wrong feet.

It was a Catholic school. I was called often.

"Mrs. Levi."

"It's Levy," I would mumble.

"Mrs. Levi, are you aware that your daughter's shoes ARE ON THE WRONG FEET?" one teacher asked.

I laughed. "Yes, she likes to wear them that way and pretend she's Donald Duck. I do put them on the correct feet before we head out in the morning."

I felt like a criminal after some of these phone calls.

I was still giving the children chores while at home. Kyle's chore was to clean his room. On one particular day, I noticed that Kyle hadn't cleaned his room.

"Kyle," I said angrily while I was cooking dinner at the stove. "You have got to clean that room. I've showed you how to do it. I mean it. You're not going to live like a pig."

I looked out from the corner of my eye to see my son pretend to shake something at me. "… compels you. The power of …," Kyle whispered.

I stopped in mid taste with a wooden spoon in my hand and stared at my son.

"Why you little stinker, are you calling me possessed????" I said as my jaw hit the floor.

He just giggled at me

Then it hit me. We had seen excerpts from "The Exorcist" the night before as a promo for the upcoming Halloween holiday.

I started to laugh and relented. I was so impressed that he put that together that I completely gave up on his cleaning the room that night. His humor was definitely improving. The weird thing was that Kyle struggled to understand jokes, but he was naturally hilarious in the way he perceived the ironies of life, even at that young age. This was a perfect example.

I began getting daily phone calls from Kyle's Kindergarten teacher on other areas of his learning. She was concerned about his behavior. He wouldn't sit still. He transitioned poorly. He fought with the other children and none of the other boys would play with him.

One boy did finally play with him after the teacher asked for a volunteer. She described the boy as a natural leader. I tried unsuccessfully to make play dates with the boy, and found the mother reluctant to let her son play with Kyle. She would hurry her son away when she saw me approach. I sensed that she was worried the association might "rub off" on her son.

My heart ached for Kyle. He seemed so lonely and I began to worry about his future for the first time. Most of the people who attended the church were warm and welcoming. Some of the mothers attending the school were not. "This is a Catholic school, for Christ's sake," I thought to myself. "You know a place where we demonstrate Christ's love in action?" I found myself grumbling under my breath.

The Kindergarten teacher became increasingly antagonistic towards me. One day, she finally confronted me.

"Miss C told me that Kyle has been assessed ADHD," she fumed.

"Yes, but I'm going to get a second opinion. Changes in his diet have been very helpful," I countered warily.

"Kyle needs to be on medication! It's criminal not to give it to him. If this continues, the authorities may need to be notified," she sniffed in disgust.

My heart raced. The threat was very clear: "Put Kyle on meds."

I was convinced that the meds only made the children more manageable for the teachers. I had told this to Rick several times and it seemed self-serving for this teacher to insist on medication. Kyle seemed so depressed that I finally relented.

I took Kyle, reluctantly, back to another Psychiatrist and he was put on medication for ADHD.

I don't know if I'll ever forgive that teacher, or myself, for putting him on medication. It is the single greatest regret of my life that I didn't hold firm in my resolve.

On the way home, we stopped off at a coffee shop. I bought Kyle a cookie and myself a cup of coffee. We sat down next to a table filled with about ten bikers. They were all wearing leather and sported piercings or tattoos. They seemed pretty fierce as they glared around the room while they fingered their chains.

Kyle looked at the bikers and then said in a voice loud enough for the entire store to hear, "Mommy, can men marry men?"

The entire table of bikers stopped talking and looked at me.

"Well, Kyle, in our society it isn't considered legal for men to marry men but we're Christians, so we don't judge," I said, absolutely horror stricken. (It was 1996, and nineteen years before the law would be changed.) As I looked up from my coffee, the biggest biker at the table nodded in appreciation. Then they all began talking again.

We finished our coffee and walked outside. When we got to the car, I knelt down next to Kyle and took his shoulders into my hands. "Kyle, you can marry anyone you want, ok?" I smiled.

Kyle smiled but couldn't think of anyone he wanted to marry.

"I'm only six!" Kyle said looking out the window while bouncing his feet.

We put Kyle on the medication Ritalin, and waited to see the results.

The medication over the next few weeks was a nightmare. Kyle wouldn't eat. He lost weight and dark circles formed under his eyes. He stared dully into space for long periods of time. I had to beg him to eat. He complained daily of stomach aches and headaches.

And then the tics came. They started with eye ticks and progressed to nasal ticks, sniffing and head jerking.

The doctors now determined he had possible Tourette's Syndrome.

I was furious! It was obvious to me that the medicines were causing the tics. I was terrified that they would become permanent which was a real possibility after reading up on the medications' side effects.

I took Kyle back to the doctor and insisted that they take him off the meds. They switched the meds several times instead, and finally the tics subsided, but he still wouldn't eat.

Kyle developed a curious habit of chewing on his clothes, particularly the top button of his shirts or his collars. Sometimes he chewed holes in the sleeve cuffs. He hated anything that chaffed his bare skin. He complained that some clothes scratched him. He was hypersensitive to all but the softest fibers. He also insisted on wearing his sunglasses constantly. He said that they helped him see. He was hypersensitive to light.

I suffered from migraines and I noticed that I was hypersensitive to light as well. I was especially vulnerable to fluorescent lights that could trigger a migraine if I was subjected to them for more than an hour. I also wore sunglasses consistently to avoid the headaches, so I didn't think anything of Kyle's comment. It actually made sense when he began having migraine headaches too.

But he was only 6 years old! I worried that the medications were giving him the headaches. I worried about the long term effects of the medications on his physical development. It seemed to me that if the teachers and doctors didn't know what was wrong, then somehow I must be responsible. My husband and I were questioned time and time again: "Was there trouble in the home? Were my husband and I fighting? Does Kyle eat healthy foods? What did you eat while pregnant with Kyle?" Round and round like a merry go round it went. I became more and more disgusted with the teacher and the medical institutions.

After a particularly grueling day, I finally voiced my frustration.

"Honestly, these doctors are no better than Medieval Butchers," I mocked. "We now know that these things are caused by an imbalance of bodily fluids and demons." My husband laughed.

"It's not funny, Rick. I'm so frustrated that I don't know what to do. He's on drugs and his teacher still seems to dislike him. She thinks I'm the problem. She takes it out on Kyle. And, there's nothing I can do about it. I'm starting to really dislike that Troll. She should be living under a bridge eating goats."

I thought it couldn't get any worse.

I was wrong.

Kyle's teacher questioned my husband one day when he picked Kyle up from school.

"Is he really on his meds?" the teacher glared.

"He's on the meds; we have some sad side effects to prove it," Rick nodded grimly.

"Well, the meds don't seem to be helping him sit still enough," she muttered aggressively.

"Listen," he responded. "He was on Ritalin and that gave him tics. They now have him on Dexedrine which is giving him headaches and he can't eat. You're telling me the meds don't work, so what am I supposed to think? Does he have ADHD or Auditory Processing disorder or not? Two weeks ago they said he had Tourette's because of the tics caused by the MEDS! Maybe MEDS aren't the answer because KYLE'S NOT THE PROBLEM."

The teacher stopped and looked blankly at Rick.

"He needs the medication," she said weakly.

"Come on, Bud, lets go," Rick said sharply as he scooped Kyle into his arms.

Rick came home disgusted.

"Donna, maybe Kyle's teacher needs the meds!"

I smiled sadly and nodded.

"Everybody seems to be an 'expert' on Kyle's condition, but nobody really knows how to help him. It's like playing Russian roulette with the drugs.... here try this one, doesn't work? Oh, okay let's try this drug and see what happens. My kid isn't going to be some fucking lab rat," Rick yelled while his hands shook in fury.

A week later I got a phone call. All hell had broken loose and her name was Sister "Daki." Since I got so many calls, I was initially unconcerned. The principal called me into her office insisting it be that very day. I reluctantly got into my car, regretting the sweats I had put on that morning for a run. I arrived completely underdressed for the Inquisition.

The principal was usually a sweet, business focused woman. I found her completely agitated as she motioned to the chair. I sat down. She proceeded to tell me about the INCIDENT involving Kyle and a nun named Sister Daki while I sank lower and lower into my chair.

Kyle was playing roughly with two other boys and a fight broke out. Sister Daki intervened and that's when it happened.

"KYLE HIT SISTER DAKI!" she spoke loudly to emphasize her point.

I blinked uncomprehendingly.

"Yes, you don't understand. It was SISTER DAKI. HE HIT SISTER DAKI! She's been a nun here for years. She even taught me when I was a child," the principal finished in a rush of words.

I finally understood. This principal was horrified by my son's actions, because she was terrified of Sister Daki, which I suspected was deeply rooted in a childhood awe or reverence.

"Wow! Okay, I want to talk to Kyle."

I found Kyle in the outer waiting room.

"Kyle?" I began.

"Mom, she was the BAD WOMAN, Mom. She grabbed me from behind so I did just what you told me. I punched her in the stomach just like Dad showed me and I ran away." He spoke rapidly in defensiveness.

I understood immediately.

I returned to the Principal and paused for a moment.

"Was Sister Daki wearing her Nun's Habit?" I questioned.

"No," she replied and seemed confused by my question.

I nodded.

"Did she identify herself as a nun, or a teacher to Kyle? I mean, did he know who she was in this school?"

"I'm not sure." The Principal chewed her lip

I crinkled my nose and smiled.

"I'd like to meet SISTER DAKI!" I said playfully widening my eyes for effect.

The Principal seemed uneasy but eventually nodded and pointed to where Sister Daki was standing outside.

Sister Daki was standing outside on the curb looking grimly into the distance. The Principal pointed to her and nodded through the window at me.

My resolve to get to the heart of the matter made me bold. "Hey Sister Daki, what's the deal? Don't you guys where habits anymore?" I asked with a grin.

"No, we don't wear those anymore," she answered as her eyes widened in surprise.

"Sister Daki, my husband is a Federal Agent. He's had several death threats against him and our family. We've always told Kyle that if a "bad man or woman" comes at him or tries to grab him, he has our permission to do whatever it takes to get away and call for help. Kyle didn't mean to hurt you, you frightened him and he didn't know who you were." I explained.

Sister Daki pondered for a moment. Her eyes went wide and then she laughed.

"Oh wow, I didn't know," Sister Daki replied.

"I'll make sure he apologizes to you," I laughed back.

Kyle apologized and gave her a hug at the knees impulsively. She seemed astonished at the hug and from that moment on, Sister Daki smiled whenever she saw us. She also took an interest in Kyle and made a point of asking how he was progressing. She actually began looking out for him on the playground. I came to really enjoy Sister Daki despite the curious looks that I got from some of the other parishioners who remained in awe of her.

I was relieved when Kyle graduated from Kindergarten. We continued working that summer and Kyle quickly learned most of the 1st grade curriculum. I was anxious that he learn how to read because he seemed to inevitably fall behind little by little. Kyle would struggle to keep up by March even though he already knew the material. He was fresh in the morning when he did his best learning. He was so mentally tired in the afternoon from all the "sensory input" that he just couldn't focus anymore.

There was another boy who struggled with the school work. He and Kyle became buddies that year. They walked to the Principal's office, hand in hand, where the school nurse gave them their meds during lunch. Kyle was medicated for the hyperactive form of Attention Deficit Disorder (ADHD) while this little boy was medicated for the milder form ADD or Attention Deficit Disorder. Kyle seemed protective over this little boy, and he seemed so pleased to have a friend like himself. They played together constantly and he was a quiet, gentle boy. Kyle blossomed through this new friendship. He even protected this boy from being bullied which made Kyle feel needed and important. I learned about this one day when I came by for an afternoon of volunteer work at the Church. Miss C saw me, called me over with a laugh and explained she had been watching both boys on the playground during recess. She said that she was impressed that Kyle would stand up to the other boys when they tried to push his friend around. I smiled and thanked Miss C for telling me the story. I said silent prayers of thanksgiving as I watched my son walk to the principles office. He had a protective arm slung over his friend's shoulder.

Kyle's friend had a birthday party at a Pizza Parlor and invited Kyle. They walked hand in hand to hug a giant toy mouse and posed for pictures. I was so happy for Kyle and relieved. I had been hoping for him to make a friend. So many people shied away from Kyle, as if he was contagious.

There were many days when I would drop Kyle off at school in the mornings only to feel the stares of the other parents. They would look at Kyle, then back at me while backing up slightly. Sometimes they would nervously look off into the distance or pretend to notice something on the ground. One morning, I encouraged Kyle to say hello to a little boy holding his mother's hand and the mother glared at me. She looked at my clothes from top to bottom and then arched an eyebrow at Kyle. I fought the urge to accept her subtle, nonverbal criticism and shook my head. She drove off in her $50,000 car and it hit me; despite the fact that this was a Catholic school, there were still people who felt superior, based on the cars they drove and the clothes they wore.

"Jesus was a CARPENTERS SON, YOU WENCH," I mumbled to myself, at which point it started to drizzle. I smiled and nodded at the rain which seemed a reflection of my mood as I left the school that day.

I met the father of Kyle's friend who told me with tears in his eyes that his sons ADD diagnosis saved his life. His son would dreamily look off into the distance and could not concentrate for more than a moment at a time. When the school suggested that his son be tested for his difficulty in focusing, the father was shocked. He had been unable to focus all his life which threatened his job, relationships and family. When his son was finally diagnosed, his father cried. "You mean there's medicine for this?" he asked the Doctor. He was tested and was found to have the same condition as his son. So, the doctor gave him a prescription and it changed his whole life. He could focus for the first time. His wife nodded as she listened to the story. "It's true. The medicine saved his life," she said with a sad smile. This little boy was doing remarkably well in his school work since he was put on the medicine. He was focused, inquisitive and receptive to the curriculum. His grades were improving and he talked more.

I was happy for him, but I still had my doubts about Kyle's diagnosis. The medicine didn't really seem to help him focus. He wasn't more verbal or receptive to his studies if there was a lot of outside stimulation. He just seemed tired and subdued. Kyle could hyper-focus without the meds on the weekends if he was interested in the subject matter. He would take apart and put back together intricate mechanical objects or toys for hours on end. Kyle was interested in very little when he was on the meds. Only his hearing improved on the medication but his mood was bleak and he complained of stomach aches. I was cynical about whether the medication was doing any good and began to doubt the diagnosis, but I was unsure what to do about it. Kyle seemed like a Zombie on the medication.

The days dragged and the weeks flew as we prepared for the fall. The leaves changed colors. The chill in the air created an atmosphere of expectancy as the children dressed for Halloween. Kyle was the "smart" Power Ranger in blue who invented scientific wonders. Caitlin was the Pink Power Ranger and kicked anyone within range with a giggle. The nuns bit their lips and questioned the costumes. Were they appropriate for a Church? Miss C just laughed and pointed out that I would be forced to tell them "no kicking" for the rest of the night.

All too soon, Kyle and Caitlin were bringing home colored turkeys made from their hand tracings. Kyle's favorite holiday is Thanksgiving. He loved helping to prepare all the food with his father and organizing all the dishes. We always made pumpkin pie the day before. I would let Kyle have a slice on the morning of Thanksgiving for breakfast with whipped cream.

We always put the Christmas tree up on Thanksgiving Day. Cat and I gather all the decorations and play Christmas music. We make hot chocolate and popcorn. We spend the day lazily putting them all up while Rick makes dinner.

That's right. I haven't made a Thanksgiving turkey... ever. Rick is a gourmet cook and I'm the luckiest woman in the world. I'm perfectly content to wash the dishes. Kyle decided that he would cook with Daddy. We later praised Kyle for the wonderful dishes he prepared.

"The ladies love a man who cooks, Kyle," Rick said with a wink as he peered at me in the living room.

"They do!" I yelled back surrounded by a mass of Christmas tree lights.

We ended the day by watching "Miracle on 34th street" while I cuddled with Cat.

We decorated for the holidays but that December was a wistful one.

I decided to put my fears to God through prayer. I prayed for three days asking God to give me a dream. I wanted a sign from God to help me cure my son of his difficulties: the right foods, or the right meds, or something... anything.

On the fourth day, I awoke from a dream and told my husband about it.

In the dream, I was living in My Fathers house and Kyle was homeless on the street sitting on the curb wearing a blue Power Ranger uniform. He looked lonely and dejected. I asked my Father (knowing it was God in the dream) if I could bring him into the house. God said, "yes." I brought him into the laundry room. I cleaned him up and fed him before it was time for him to sleep. Then I woke up.

I understood completely.

There was no medicine, or food, or program that I could obtain that would cure Kyle. I was meant to help Kyle just by giving him a safe place to rest from the world. He was going to be a great thinker and inventor who would help the world someday. (The Blue Power Ranger was a scientist and smart as well as sweet.)

I felt a sense of peace and calm after the dream. It made perfect sense and I said a prayer of thanks.

Several months prior to this dream, Rick had put in for a transfer overseas. He had originally been assigned to India, but then had his heart procedure, so the transfer had been cancelled. He had put in for other transfers as well, but we forgot about them during the stress of his recovery.

He was completely recovered and received a phone call from Headquarters. Was he still interested in an overseas position as a consultant? My husband said yes and accepted a new job. We would soon be leaving Spokane, Washington.

Rick left for most of the year to attend language school held in Washington D.C. He flew home once a month for a long weekend here and there, but the distance was grueling. We decided to live apart for the children's schooling since Kyle was actually starting to see some real progress. We thought the disruption of two moves in 18 months would do more harm than good, especially for him.

Rick finally finished with school and returned home for the holidays.

We were going to Thailand!

CHAPTER 6

International School Bullies

My husband was transferred to Chiang Mai, Thailand that year for a training position with the Thai police. Chiang Mai was located in the Mountains of Thailand. We said bittersweet goodbyes to everyone and prepared for an exciting adventure.

I took Kyle and Caitlin to the State park by the Spokane River. We decided to have one last picnic before we went to Thailand. It was a short picnic because of the cold. The day was sunny, despite the cold, and some of the trees still had brown leaves on them that waved in the wind. I said, "Let's just drive through the park since it's so chilly out there. OK?" The sky was a deep blue and the river sparkled under the sun. I was daydreaming about the move and silently clicking off boxes in my head over all the things we needed to accomplish. I would miss the thick woods in the park despite the fact there had been a fire several years before. Many of the trees were blackened and bent from that fire. I pointed out birds and a fox running low to the ground. I saw an Eagle perched on top of a telephone poll. Kyle stared round eyed at the Eagle while Caitlin tried to stand and look down into the river.

"Enjoy this beautiful view, because this is our last day to

drive through the park," I said with a sad smile. "Maybe we should cross the river and see the rest of the park. What do you think?"

As we were driving, Kyle became very afraid.

"Mom, we can't go in there because there are bad Indians in there!" Kyle whispered.

"What Bad Indians? Kyle, who told you about Bad Indians?" I asked horrified.

"My friends told me at school, Mom," Kyle countered defensively.

I was silent for a moment.

"Kyle, are we bad people?" I asked quietly.

"No."

"Kyle, we're Indian," I said.

Kyle looked at his arms and shook his head violently.

"Uh uh….we're not Indian," He was vehement.

"Kyle, my grandmother was Cherokee. We are descendents of the Cherokee nation. You are Irish, Scot, French, Dutch, German, English and INDIAN!!!" I finally said in exasperation. "Kyle, I want you to understand and appreciate who you are and where you come from. I also want you to accept ALL of who you are and not just little bits and pieces. Yes, you look like my mother who resembled the French side of our family. Cat looks English and I look like I'm right off the boat from Ireland. That still doesn't change our history, Honey."

Kyle continued to look at his skin in wonder. He just couldn't get over the color of his skin and reconcile this to his image of a Native American. He didn't look Native American so he couldn't possibly BE Native.

I wondered how he could have heard such prejudice at

such early an age and shook my head in disgust.

"Maybe it's a good idea that we're going to a foreign country to an International school so that Kyle can meet people from all kinds of backgrounds," I thought to myself. I want him to have a real education in different cultures.

We left Spokane that winter for Thailand.

We arrived after a 15 hour, sleepless flight. We played games and the children colored in their coloring books. I had brought a silver bell that played music. Kyle would hold it and listen to it until he fell asleep. Both the children climbed over our laps to look out the plane windows. They took turns putting the head phones on and off. We played cards and I hugged them frequently to comfort my own nervousness.

Our layover in Tokyo was unnerving as we sat on our luggage waiting for the next flight to Bangkok. The people stared at us in the Tokyo airport, and on the plane to Bangkok. The staring never stopped.

When we arrived in Thailand, it was Durian season. Durian is called the "King" fruit. It's the size of a football, tastes like a fruity onion with the consistency of an avocado. It's actually delicious. The smell, however, is so hideously rotten that restaurants won't let you bring it indoors. That's right–the smell in the air, everywhere, was akin to decaying road kill. I was thrilled as I walked through the streets holding my breath.

Still, there were so many amazing sights and sounds to experience. Thai people seemed very friendly. They would come up and touch the children. They marveled at Caitlin's purple-blue eyes. Young teenage girls would come up to Caitlin and put their fingers through her hair and giggle. Sometimes they would call her "Suii", which means pretty. Some of the adults would pinch Kyle's arms or stomach and say "Uuon", which means fat or "well fed and affluent." Kyle found all this very agitating. He would growl or retreat into his own world.

The night markets and malls are very loud with advertisements, all speaking over each other. The competing sounds made Kyle dreamy, and he would retreat into himself while rocking or moving his legs rhythmically. The lights were mesmerizing to Kyle, and he would stare into space. He could only handle an hour of this and then he would begin to shut down. Sometimes he became hyper and hypersensitive if you spoke to him. Other times he would get angry and lash out or cry.

We settled into a neighborhood that had other American families. There were children on "The Compound" as we called it. Kyle and Caitlin stayed together when they played with the other children. Caitlin protected Kyle often during this time. There were several bullies who lived there and they seemed to delight in torturing Kyle. I would watch from my window as they played. As amusing as they found Kyle to tease, they were equally afraid of Cat and her temper, if the bullying went too far. "She really was born for you, Kyle," I thought silently one day as I watched them play.

We found an International school. The headmaster seemed friendly and the school had a warm, casual feel. We were fortunate to find that one of the teachers had been a speech therapist. She seemed pleased with the idea of helping Kyle and keeping her professional skill level current. We engaged her to work with Kyle after school. Kyle seemed to like her sweetness and her warmth. She worked with him for only a few months, since we arrived in Chiang Mai in early March. A few months later summer break arrived.

I home schooled Kyle that summer. Reading regular books was a nightmare for him. He just got lost in the maze of squiggled lines on the pages. He could read short sentences if I broke them up individually. I began reading a book on snakes that had more pictures than words and had the text running under the picture, or on the side. If the sentences were four lines or less, it seemed to help him. When we worked on spelling, I had to walk him around the room vocalizing the sequence of letters. Sometimes, I put these to rhythms, like rap, and that seemed to help. As long as he was moving, he was able to do it.

"R. E. D. RED, R. E. D. RED," he would rap while dancing to the beat, or "Yel-low, Yel-low," and clap his hands. Sometimes, I would put the words to the music of a popular song. We would practice his spelling every afternoon, once school started, in the fading light of our living room. It was the hardest class for him. He struggled at school, as well, and it affected his behavior.

He became more nervous. He started to bite his nails, his shirts and his buttons. He had a nervous sniff when he was confused. My father had the same mannerism, so I didn't think much of it at the time. I just assumed he would grow out of it.

We would go to the Catholic Mass on Sundays where we sat on Tatami mats. Sometimes Kyle would fidget so much that the other parishioners would glare at us. After all, "what was WRONG with us that we couldn't control our child?"

I pulled Kyle aside one day and said, "Kyle STOP ROCKING. You're disturbing everyone!"

He looked up at me with a crushed expression on his face.

"Mom, I can't feel my body if I don't move. I don't feel connected to it unless I'm moving." Kyle whispered.

I was horrified at my own lack of compassion under the weight of all those condemning stares. I apologized. "I'm sorry, Kyle. I didn't know," I said shaking my head. I was deeply ashamed of myself. I let Kyle rock in church after that, and ignored the stares we got from some people.

That following summer we struggled with so many things: new culture, new language and the summer home schooling. Reading continued to be the most difficult for Kyle.

Then, one day, I found Kyle reading one of my college text books on Biology. Biology!

"Hey, Bud, what have you got there?" I asked.

"Look, Mom. It says that there is a small In test tine and a BIG In test tine. It's where your poop comes from!"

"What? You can read that Kyle?"

"Yeah…well it has nice pictures and the words aren't all squashed together," Kyle explained.

Sure enough. I looked at the pages and most of the text was 2-4 sentences followed by pictures of some sort. I was floored, because it was college level reading. I had him read 2 pages to me. He stumbled on the bigger words, asking for definitions that I simplified to an 8 year old level. But he read everything else clearly.

I was dumbfounded. Kyle wasn't smart, he was brilliant! He could read a college text book. He also had an almost photographic memory when he read something that interested him. I realized that he didn't see the information the same way most people did, and he didn't process information in the same way either. His thinking was more circular, where concepts were "impressed" by large chunks rather than linear individual words. He read the words skipping around from line to line, up and down, first back, then forth, and then sometimes back again within a circle. I had to figure out a way to reach him. He loved Science and Math, so I started bringing home books that I could use to help him read: Astronomy, Robotics, Reptiles, and Mechanics. He especially loved Engineering. I kept the lessons short and he sailed through them, as long as they had interesting pictures.

He started 2nd grade that August.

I left Thailand shortly after that to study for a Masters in Social Work. Rick and I had decided that I would go back to school, so that he could retire early due to his heart disease. I would then work while he played "Mr. Mom." It seemed perfect since we were able to hire a full time maid/nanny for the children, and Rick worked across the street. We were told that his job would be a desk job for the most part. I would come home Christmas and summers.

"This is an opportunity of a lifetime... you have to go. I don't care what the neighbors think," Rick said, rolling his eyes for emphasis. "I'll get a full time maid to help me with the kids. It'll be fine. I'll try to coordinate our home leave times to visit you in Spokane, too. We'll work it out."

The first six months, I cried everyday. I came home on holidays and the following summer, but I was torn. I needed an education in case Rick had another heart attack. We couldn't survive on a medical retirement. Still, the geographical distance strained our marriage, and we became emotionally distant with each other. I needed the education so I went, but I felt that, despite his support, Rick began to resent my absence. It was stressful communicating with him long distance over the phone. There were long silences. I loved the work, but felt terribly guilty about leaving Kyle and Caitlin. They were so little. I wrote every day and called once a week to talk to them. It wasn't enough, but I knew it was only for 2 years. Our conversations were always about the kids.

Rick purchased a computer and called me one night excited. Kyle could zip through his homework in half the time on the computer.

Why?

He was moving, using his fingers on the key board. The screen moved and changed, but slowly, so that Kyle wasn't overwhelmed. He could hyper-focus on the screen and it kept him engaged. So Rick tutored Kyle on the computer. "Wait till you see him work when you come home," Rick laughed.

I came home that Christmas to spend the holidays with the family. I also came home to the glares of some of the other mothers. The full time homemaker's made it very clear: "I was a terrible mother to leave my children," and some even said so to my face under the guise of "helpful" concern.

"You don't realize how hard it's going to be after a while," said one mother while rolling her eyes to one side.

"REAL mothers don't leave their children," said another mother, self righteously.

Another mother walked away smiling maliciously as she nodded her head.

Only one mother understood. She taught the deaf and was studying Thai language herself. She smiled kindly to me and then looked uncomfortably at the other mothers.

Rick was also feeling the pressure. Some of the men in his office grilled him.

"Well, why did you let her go?"

"If she were my wife, there would be no way. She's never coming back. "

"Thanks, now my wife is nagging me to go back to school."

Rick grumbled through gritted teeth, "I can't chain her to the tree in the backyard."

We commiserated but were determined to enjoy the holidays. On Christmas morning, Kyle came into our bedroom excited. We had spent a late night at an Embassy party on Christmas Eve and were still half asleep.

"Mom, Dad, wake up! It's Christmas," he said while pulling on the covers of our bed.

"Oh, Bud," Rick groaned. "Go and get Grandma's present. You can open that one and we'll be right down."

"I'll make the coffee," I said groggily as I hid my head back under my pillow.

Kyle opened the present from Grandma and then came running back to our room. I buried my head deeper under the pillow.

"Mom, Grandma got me a Robot. Will you help me put it together?" Kyle asked breathlessly jumping up and down.

I looked at the time and it was 5 am. I groaned.

"Okay, Buddy, in a few minutes." I heard Rick mumble.

A few minutes later, we heard whirring, beeping and whizzing. We sat up and quietly made our way to the bedroom door. We looked outside and a small robot was walking past with lights flashing. Kyle had put the Robot together just by looking at the schematics. We watched in awe as it walked across the room.

Kyle had made Caitlin a doll house that Christmas complete with pulleys and elevators. He had transformed a

WHERE THE ORCHID BLOOMS

cardboard box into a "Hotel" and had colored the different rooms, adding stairs and windows. It was a marvel, and Cat loved it.

That wasn't the only gift Kyle gave Cat that year. He spent most of his saved up allowance to buy her a small cut glass dog he found in the street market while shopping with our maid, "Khun D". The dog was no bigger than a quarter. He knew she loved trinkets to look at on a windowsill or bookshelf, and that she loved animals. He knew this was also the perfect gift to go with the hotel. He wrapped it in red Christmas paper and placed it carefully under the tree.

On Christmas morning, when all the presents had been opened, the wrapped dog wasn't there. Cat didn't know he had bought her a second gift, and didn't know why Kyle was so upset. He was on his hands and knees under the Christmas tree, throwing ripped wrapping paper over the room searching for that glass dog. Kyle was devastated.

"Kyle, don't worry, whatever you're looking for will turn up. You'll see. Probably when we take down the tree and clean this place," Cat said to cheer him up, still not knowing the gift was for her.

"Yeah..." Kyle said sadly, not looking her in the eye.

"Come on dude, it's Christmas! Let's watch 'It's a Wonderful Life' with mom," Cat said tugging on his shirt leading him to the family room. This is a family tradition every year. On Christmas Eve we eat fun finger foods and watch Dickens' "A Christmas Carol." This reminds us to share and bring joy to others on Christmas. On Christmas day we open presents and then watch "It's a Wonderful Life". This reminds us of all our blessings and that everyone makes a difference in other people's lives.

A week later while taking down the tree, Cat found the wrapped gift under one of the chairs that was on the side of the tree. Christmas came twice for her that year, and she loved that glass dog.

During the kids' Christmas holidays we took the time to explore the mountains of Thailand. We visited the snake farm and Kyle was mesmerized by the snake handlers. The handlers barely escaped being bitten by the Cobras. We visited the elephant farm and watched the baby elephants play in the rivers. We went to a zoo where a camel came up to the edge of the wall and put his head on Kyle's shoulder. We went to the butterfly farm and I watched in amazement as dozens of butterflies landed on Kyle's arms and shoulders. He would stand there patiently, quietly watching them. It was one of the few times that Kyle and time seemed to stand still. It was magical.

This inspired Kyle to reach out to other kids about his knowledge of snakes. He knew so much that the Kindergarten teacher asked him to come and speak to her class. Kyle was excited to do so and agreed. Kyle received an award during that time for going into the Kindergarten class on his lunch hour and teaching them about snakes. The principal gave him the award in a sweet ceremony commending his hard work and everyone clapped. My husband took pictures of the ceremony and sent me copies. I was so happy for Kyle. He proudly hung that award on his wall.

"So, how's it going?" I asked Rick one day after I returned to the States to continue my studies.

"It's good. I come home from work and usually take them swimming at the pool. In the beginning, when you left, the kids took it pretty hard. I started taking them swimming and then would help them with their homework until dinner. Khun D is a godsend. She cleans and cooks, which takes the pressure off of me. I take them on the weekends somewhere to see the sights. I take them to the Night Bazaar sometimes and we see toys or the food on sale. When Kyle has had enough and starts to "shut down", then I take them home. We bought Kyle a preserved Tarantula the other day. We found a German Restaurant and an English pub where we like to go for dinner. Oh, and I take them for ice cream at the airport. They love it... real American food," he laughed.

"The only real American food is at the Airport, so I take them once a week. Last week we had chili dogs and watched the airplanes. I'll take them next week to get a 'Samurai Pork Burger' or Thai chili pizza."

"Wow," I countered.

"Most of the time, we just give Khun D the weekend off if I'm not working, and the kids cook with me," Rick said. "School is a little strange."

"Why?" I was alarmed.

"Well, I went to a Parent-Teacher conference the other day. Kyle's teacher said he was doing just fine in his studies."

"What is he struggling with in school that we need to work on?" I countered.

"Exactly. He said there was nothing to worry about," Rick said disgusted.

"That doesn't sound right." I was really concerned now.

"Well, how is his homework going?" I asked confused.

"That's the point. He doesn't have homework." Rick paused and said, "I asked him what he was learning the other day, and he said he spent most of the time drawing or playing. I've talked to the other parents and some of the other teachers.

Kyle's teacher is suffering from depression."

"That's not our problem. He has a job to do!" I was starting to get angry.

"I know, I'll handle it," Rick said grimly.

I came home later that summer. It was obvious that he had learned very little the previous year. He was so far behind. Kyle continued to need little help in Math, but he was becoming more and more behind in reading. My home schooling became a battle. I decided that the kids might do better with someone they felt was a "real" teacher. We finally hired a tutor named "J" to tutor both children that summer. Kyle and Caitlin adored her. She was gentle, kind and completely focused. Both the children thrived under her care. I still helped with the "homework".

We would go to the Night Bazaar on the weekends, especially if Kyle worked hard on his school work. He always gravitated towards the "bug" table. There were an assortment of moths, spiders, scorpions and butterflies. They were huge compared to some of our American species. Kyle was fascinated by them and acquired several to hang on his wall.

We were horrified a few weeks later when, inside the frame, tiny bugs crawled out of the specimens. They had never been properly prepared and preserved, so these bugs had been feeding on the carcasses under the glass. We eventually convinced Kyle to throw them away.

I began cooking from scratch because many foods we loved couldn't be found in Thailand until a few years later. We made homemade tortillas and bagels. (The bagels never really turned out.) Sometimes the maid, Khun D, would laugh at our cooking.

"Farong-bua," Khun D said, pointing to the food. "Foreign

food is boring," she would say with a smile until one night we made homemade Mexican food. The food was extra spicy and Khun D loved it. After that day we always made a plate for her when we made Mexican food.

I headed back to my second year in the Social Work Masters program. I learned so many valuable things about systems: schools, hospitals, groups and individuals. I learned too many things to name with one exception. The most valuable thing that I learned is that people build on their strengths. Find their passion and you will find the key to their success. Everyone resists change, even when they initiate it, and the key to walking people through change is by holding their hand while they determine the way. This became the single most important theme in my reaching Kyle.

Becoming a Social Worker made me a better mother. I eventually came back with a renewed sense of optimism and determination in helping Kyle. I was also determined not to allow myself to be cowed by so called "experts". Many of the doctors and educators had a cursory interest in Kyle at best. Many of them seemed to find comfort in having quick answers. It seemed that it made them feel in control. While some of them were well meaning, they were not always helpful to Kyle's development in the long run. They also always seemed to concentrate on what he FAILED to do or COULDN'T do, rather than on what he COULD accomplish. They always underestimated his potential. Of course, I've come to the conclusion that control is an illusion. I mean, when a mosquito carrying Dengue fever can kill you, how much control do you really have?

I graduated that summer with a Masters in Social work.

Rick and the kids came to the States to visit. Rick had scheduled another heart procedure. The doctors found that the first stint was failing and another had to be inserted. The recovery was slow and Rick seemed more depressed than usual. Communication between us was tense and guarded, polite and superficial. He resented me, and I resented him in return. I felt that I was working hard to learn to provide for our family. I felt tremendous pressure to succeed and, aside from the lip service of support, I felt he was hiding from me in an emotional blanket of hidden rage.

I was also sad and frightened by the physical weakness he suffered from the surgeries.

I think that my attitude affected both children, especially Kyle.

Rick asked Kyle to do something one day after the surgery. Kyle mouthed off in a way that was so disrespectful, I just lost it.

Before I knew what I was doing, I pulled my arm back and slapped him across the face with a force I didn't know was possible. Kyle fell back from the dinner table onto the floor, his chair sliding out from under him.

He looked horrified.

I began to cry. I heard myself scream, "Don't you ever, EVER talk to your father again in that disrespectful manner"! Do you HEAR me? As God is my witness, you WILL show your father RESPECT, PERIOD."

I left the dinner table and went outside. I was smoking again and lit a cigarette to calm my nerves.

I took Kyle aside later that night. "Kyle, I'm sorry I hit you. It was wrong and I lost my temper. You cannot talk to your father like that, especially when he's so sick. He's sick and weak from the surgeries. We've got to help him, Honey," I whispered.

Kyle nodded and the tears ran down his face. He buried his face into my shoulder the way he had done so many years ago when he was a baby. We just sat there and cried together. I think we both felt ashamed.

We began taking trips to Coeur D'Alene, Idaho for picnics on the beach and hikes along the lake. I thought it would cheer us all up and remind us of all the times we had spent there when the children were babies.

Coeur D'Alene is a resort town about an hour east of Spokane, WA. The town surrounds a beautiful deep water lake. The lake has hiking trails around most of it, while across the lake, there are houses that can only be reached by boat. There are plane and boat rides, parks and hiking. The town hosts ice cream parlors, Specialty T-shirt shops and homemade fudge. It also has a marina and the Coeur D'Alene resort where we dined on a 5 star Sunday brunch.

Kyle and Caitlin took a plane ride over the lake with their father, as I waved from the ground. We hiked along the lake after brunch. We marveled at the boats moored at the docks.

We returned to Washington State and took them to the State Fair. I also took them to River Front Park, where they played on the giant sled and rode the Carousel horses. And I finally took them to a Powwow with some of my Native American friends. My friends were Colville Indian, Flat head, Blackfoot Sioux and Cherokee.

When I introduced Caitlin to one of my closest friends, Lorraine who is Blackfoot Sioux and Flat Head, she laughed. "Look, she's trying to see if I have BLACK FEET," Lorraine said while pointing to Cat.

Her daughter had made a beautiful beaded purse to sell at the Powwow. I purchased it for Cat instead. It was a work of art and so tightly beaded. It was a butterfly on a tree branch. Lorraine beaded a love gift for me of a medicine bag that same day, which I still cherish. The goodbyes were bittersweet and heartwarming that summer.

I came back to Thailand after graduating with my M.S.W. just in time. Kyle started 4th grade that year and he began being bullied by several boys in the class. His teacher was compassionate and a deeply intuitive woman from Myanmar. She realized that Kyle could do the same work as everyone else, but not at the same pace. She decided that as long as he got the answers, she didn't care about the volume. He could do one page for every two pages the other kids finished. I will always be grateful for her tireless efforts on Kyle's behalf. I swore she was an angel sent to us from God. Kyle became more confident as he mastered the work she gave him.

I was called into the Principals office one day about the bullying. He explained that he had found Kyle trying to climb the ladder to the roof. When he asked Kyle for an explanation, Kyle told him that he was going to jump off the roof. He was tired and frustrated about being bullied.

I felt a cold rage when I heard that news. In my protective-ness over my son, I told the Principal that the bullying had to stop. These things only escalated in my experience until someone intervened. I insisted on a meeting with the one boy (the instigator) and his parents. We met. The boy's mother was a teacher at the school. I had had a chance to calm down by that time and really think about what I was hoping to accomplish.

I explained that I wasn't interested in punishing her son.

What I wanted was for both boys to understand the seriousness of the situation and learn about boundaries. What is and is not acceptable behavior, communication and physical contact.

After talking with "K", I realized that her son was struggling with some traumatic health issues and was acting out. We both decided that the boys would benefit from some structured play time and agreed to get together to oversee the interactions.

We did. Two things happened.

The boy's mother, K, and I became friends. Kyle and her son learned to play together and became friends.

And, secondly, I was offered a job.

The owner of the school had watched me handle the situation and told the Principal that she wanted him to hire me.

"Really?" I asked him.

"Yeah. She insisted that I come over here and offer you a job. She wants you to be a teacher here. What if you substitute this year and, if it works out, I'll offer you the Assistant Director of the Kindergarten program?" John asked. "You'll teach level 3 Kindergarten."

"Okay," I agreed, not believing my good fortune.

I came home and told Rick the good news. The distance between us had continued, even after I had come home. He nodded but didn't really say much. Since I had come back to Thailand, it seemed like he was gone all the time. He was supposed to have a relatively stable desk job, but every weekend he was headed to the jungle.

And he wasn't the only one. I had overheard one of the other wives complain that the desk job was a "bill of goods" and if she had known, she would never have come to Thailand. The men were gone for weeks and weeks at a time.

I received news that I had gotten a job in Seattle, Washington a few weeks later. Rick and I were discussing the transfer he had put in for Seattle, as well, when my daughter Cat came into the kitchen. She heard about my job and burst into tears. She just stood there sobbing.

I was horrified. I took her in my arms and assured her that I would never leave her again. I then walked over to the garbage and threw the job announcement away.

"You see? I'm not going to take the job. I promise I'll never leave you again," I said holding her until she stopped crying. She finally stopped and hugged my knees as I stood up.

I watched her run out the door to play with her friends.

"I thought you said that if you turned down a government job, you were black listed." Rick shook his head and narrowed his eyes.

"I did. I understand that one of my professors recommended me for the job. At least that's what I was told by a friend of mine," I answered as I chewed my lip realizing what I had done.

We were silent for a moment.

"Well?" Rick asked uncertainly.

"I can't leave her again. We don't know if you're going to get that job in Seattle. You've been told you're a 'shoo in' but nothing is guaranteed. I just have to have faith that there will be other jobs. I'll take the substitute job that I've been offered and see if it turns into the Assistant Director position next year," I said quietly.

Rick nodded.

We began to talk.

We started slowly at first over the next several months, trying to find our way back to some semblance of the relationship we had before moving to Thailand.

One of the things we both agreed on was that we had to work together to help Kyle. If we didn't work together, he wasn't going to make it in any area: social, academic or emotional. He was struggling terribly in every area. It became clear that one of us had to have a routine schedule to help him with his academics. Teaching was the perfect solution.

I spent the rest of the year helping Kyle with his homework, and working part-time on call as a substitute teacher.

Rick and I worked slowly to heal our relationship and we become a family again.

At the end of the school year, the Principal offered me the full time teaching position of level 3 Kindergarten. Levels 1 and 2 were preschool and I would be his Assistant Program Director of all three levels. I could help make policy and work on the curriculum for American certification the following year.

It was a dream job and a Godsend. We would live on my salary and use Rick's salary to pay off the school debt, as well as save money for our return to the States.

Most important, though, would be my presence in the school. I could spend more time with my children and help guide them with a greater understanding of the school: personalities, politics and the curriculum.

For the next year, both my children would visit me in my classroom. My students loved these visits. They would often run up to Kyle or Cat and hug their knees as a group. I loved hearing the giggles from my students and see the gratified look on my children's faces. Sometimes they would come in and read books to my students or show them interesting things. I assured both my children at different times, that they would be wonderful teachers. They seemed happy that I was present in the school.

I felt completely blessed and content when they visited.

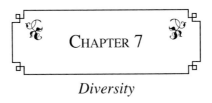

CHAPTER 7

Diversity

Kyle and I had long talks about compassion. I shared with him that he wasn't the only person who had troubles, sharing some of the struggles that other children face: poverty, disease, racism, sexism and violence. Kyle told me one day that one of the other boys had tried to touch him inappropriately, claiming he was gay.

I emphasized that Kyle had every right to say, "No, that doesn't feel comfortable to me–please stop."

"It would be the same if it was a girl who touched you and you didn't feel the same way she did. Just say, 'Thank you, I'm flattered but I don't feel the same. I'm sorry,'" I encouraged.

I cautioned him not to judge all gay people based on the actions of one boy. Caitlin listened silently to our conversation.

Caitlin came home several days later after playing with some of the other kids on the compound.

"I hate Gay people!" she shouted.

"Do you KNOW any Gay people?" I countered raising my eyebrows for mock affect.

"No," she paused thoughtfully.

"Okay, let's make some popcorn and watch a movie, "I said enthusiastically.

"Yea!" Caitlin yelled.

We watched "The Bird Cage", starring Robin Williams and Nathan Lane.

When the movie was finished, Caitlin turned to me and asked, "Are those Gay people?"

I nodded, "Some gay people."

"Gay people are funny, Mommy! I like Gay people," she giggled.

I laughed and gave her a hug. "Now, don't tell anyone we had popcorn before dinner," I said and kissed her nose.

"My little contribution to World Peace," I thought as I watched her go out to play.

Kyle came to me several days later.

"Mom, you know that guy who was always touching me and bothering me?" Kyle asked.

I nodded.

"Well, he's actually cool. He's very respectful towards me now and the three of us have been hanging out." Kyle seemed surprised.

"I'm glad, honey. You know, you don't have to understand gay people, or even agree with their lifestyle. The important thing is that you respect their right to live as they choose and not judge. We don't have to 'Get it'. We just have to have good manners, be respectful, be polite, live and let live. Because God has a sense of humor and the first time you say 'Oh I'd never BE that, or DO that', guess what? God says, 'OH YEAH? Let's see how YOU handle this situation'. I'm a little superstitious: Karma, reap what you sow, what goes around comes around, etc."

"You're a LOT superstitious," Kyle laughed.

"That doesn't mean I'm wrong." I playfully rubbed his

head with my fingers.

I smiled inwardly, grateful that this turned into a success story. It took months of careful, sometimes painfully slow reinforcement, non-judgmental accountability, and firm support to help these boys learn to get along and have respect for each other. There were times when I wasn't sure if it would ultimately work. K and I would compare notes on how the boys' interactions were progressing. I just always hoped that some good would come out of this situation for all the boys involved in the bullying. I was also, very grateful for all of K's efforts as well.

I was amazed at this wonderful friend I had found because we cooperated with each other rather than becoming adversarial to protect our sons.

I was thrilled with the prospect of working in my children's school. I was able to spend more time with them and teach them about conflict resolution, self respect and the ability to say "No" in a way that felt safe. I felt that I had to make it up to them for the two years I had been gone.

I began home schooling Kyle again that summer. It was during this time that we ran out of his ADHD medicine. We weren't able to order any more of it for six weeks because our insurance company wanted a new evaluation.

It was during those six weeks that I noticed that Kyle learned at exactly the same rate off the meds as he did on the meds. He actually retained the information better as long as we did the reading in the morning, because he was just too mentally tired by the afternoon.

When Rick came home one night, I blew up.

"Rick, I am convinced that the meds only serve to keep Kyle quiet. He's miserable. He won't eat and these drugs don't help him learn. Look, his handwriting is actually better off the meds," I seethed.

"So what do you want to do?" Rick braced himself for the answer.

"I'm taking him off these meds. He doesn't have ADHD. If he did, these things would help him. They don't and I'm done," I said grimly determined. "I'll just work harder with him on the weekends and summers. When he's ahead to start, I'll help him keep up."

My husband agreed that we would have him re-evaluated when we came home to the United States after his tour was finished in two years.

We spent that summer working hard to master the following year's curriculum. I was grateful when the dark circles began disappearing from under Kyle's eyes. He began to eat and put on weight.

It was during this time that I bought Kyle a pair of tennis shoes that had skates in the soles. It was the latest craze for kids. He loved them and skated around the neighborhood. He wore them everywhere until one day he tried skating over a speed bump.

He broke his arm.

We rushed him to the hospital. I grumbled about being in a hospital, in the mountains, in the middle of nowhere. The week before I had gone to a doctor who didn't speak English, and I didn't speak sufficient Thai. I ended up pointing and moaning. I wondered out loud what kind of witch doctor I was going to have to pantomime and sign language with this time to help my son. An Asian doctor walked out to brief us on Kyle's condition. He was a Harvard graduate with impeccable manners and he was better educated than I was.

Yep! It seems God has a sense of humor with me too. (The giant thumping sound is me being whacked over the head for my own snap judgements). I felt completely chastised and chewed my lip as we listened to the Dr. explain Kyle's condition. Rick tried hard not to laugh at me, but we both became concerned when we found that his arm was broken.

When the Doctor left, I warily glanced at Rick.

"Don't say it, just don't say it!" I mumbled.

"He speaks better English than we do," Rick chuckled.

We brought Kyle home the next day after his surgery. I made him chicken soup, Rick bought him some candy and we all signed his cast.

Caitlin was really good about helping him and I found them curled up together at night watching movies.

I remembered how Kyle and Cat started school that year, walking into school together. I began my first day of teaching as I watched them walk together, encouraging each other. I kissed my kids goodbye and walked into my Kindergarten classroom.

"Oh my God, what have I gotten myself into?" I thought as I looked around the room.

One kid was jumping up and down on my desk. One child was chasing another child with a toy snake. One boy's hands were around another boy's neck squeezing the life out of him. One child was asleep in the corner next to a boy that was crying.

Need I go on?

I yelled at the top of my lungs, "QUIET."

They all stopped and stared at me.

I walked to the front of the class, wrote my name on the

blackboard –"Ms. Donna"–and made each one repeat it.
For one week, all we worked on was manners 101.

"Excuse me, Ms. Donna, and Excuse me, Ms. Donna"
was our daily refrain. Not "hey you, Red Lady (because of
my Red hair) or Mother mine", just "Excuse me, so and so".

I drove home one day, particularly exhausted. My husband
handed me a glass of wine.

"How was it?" he asked.

"Good, but there's one kid who is smart and sweet. The
thing is: how is it that he can say my name and make it sound
like an expletive deleted?" I muttered. "'EXCUSE ME MS.
DUN- NAAAAAAA!' he says in mock disgust as he rolls
around in his chair, wildly looking at everything but me."

My husband laughed.

One of the high school students walked into class a few
weeks later. She said, "Oh Donna." I stopped the class.

"Now, what is the polite way to address an adult?" I asked
the class.

"Excuse me, Ms. Donna." The class responded.

"Yes. That's very good, class," I responded. With a smile
and a wave of my hand, I made the high school student go
out into the hall and try it again, much to her horror.

I found out later from K that some of the high school kids
were afraid of me, which was comical because I was the H.S.
student body advisor.

We settled down to a mutual, respectful understanding
after the first week, and I grew to love those children as
my own.

Kyle began coming to my classroom during his lunch
hour. The kids loved him and would scream his name when
they saw him come through the door. They would run to

him and throw their arms around his legs, hanging on him as he tried to walk. He was growing tall, at this time, and he would laugh when they hugged him while looking up at him. He would gently hug them back and show him his new book: snakes, dinosaurs, trains and airplanes.

He was a natural teacher, and I told him so again one day after I had watched him. We decided afterward to go out onto the playground. A boy called to him and Kyle just kept walking. The boy seemed hurt that Kyle didn't notice or respond.

I asked Kyle about it later and he swore that he hadn't heard the boy say "hello."

I realized that Kyle didn't seem to key on social cues at a distance, while being hyper-sensitive to body language up close.

He said to me one day, "Why are you smiling when you're so angry?"

I had been angry a few minutes earlier, dealing with a snidely nasty teacher who had called my daughter a "mediocre" student. I explained to Kyle that I was angry and he was right. I was just trying to maintain my emotions through a smile, apparently, unsuccessfully.

I told Rick later, "There are no mediocre students, only mediocre teachers. This woman actually prides herself on being a hard teacher. She hasn't the imagination or energy to be creative. She hides behind an attitude of superior pseudo-intellectualism to justify torturing little kids. Creepy little control freak."

My husband hugged me. I spoke with Caitlin later.

"Caitlin, don't let this woman tell you who you are or what you can do," I said as I put my hand on her shoulder.

"She made the whole class have a mock trial with a jury to pronounce sentence on me because she accused me of stealing an eraser, Mom. She found the eraser the next day and never apologized to me," Caitlin said through her tears.

I hugged her hard. My heart ached for her and there was nothing I could do about it without making it worse for her. I was convinced anything I did would only antagonize the situation, but Caitlin and I talked everyday about her feelings on the class. I started tutoring her more on the weekends. Cat was bright, but her spirit was cowed by this experience. I began reading to her at night the AMERICAN GIRL series and NANCY DREW thinking that she could relate to being a "hero" in every story. I hoped it would give her confidence. Her grades began to improve slowly and I ignored this teacher during P.T.A. meetings.

Cat began coming to my classroom on the lunch hour too, and the children in my class loved her as well. She would play with them and tell them stories, or read to them as I read to her. I watched her on one particular day and felt such pride in her.

"Cat, you're so gentle and kind to children. You are the kind of person who SHOULD be teaching. You would be creative and fun while still holding your students to a high standard. You should think about becoming a teacher someday." I smiled as I pushed a strand of hair from her eyes.

This was one of the best years of my life, being so close to both my children. The days in Thailand at the International school passed languidly and sweetly in the tropical heat.

K suggested that Kyle might be dyslexic since he more readily understood concepts in 3 dimensional form. She said that the U.K. dyslexics were being taught using clay models because they got lost reading letters on 2 dimensional papers. K herself was dyslexic and often transposed her letters and numbers. She used colored paper to help her read more easily. She often struggled when adding long columns of numbers. I was humbled and grateful for the time she took to assess my son and the subsequent sharing of that confidence. We talked while watching the School festivities.

It was now Chinese New Year. We watched the celebration with the lucky Chinese dragon manned by several people, playfully scaring the little children. As the fire crackers went off, K offered to tutor Kyle. She would try these new techniques for Dyslexics and see if there was any improvement. I gratefully accepted.

We both began trying these techniques, K at school and me at home.

The information she gave me was fascinating. She stated that for many Dyslexics, thinking is actually outside of themselves in a 3 dimensional orientation. They will see 2 dimensional objects from above and behind or below, and describe these accurately. They have trouble and often turn the letters or numbers upside down or backwards because they see these things from all the angles.

After several months of tutoring, K decided that "something else is afoot."

I agreed. Some of the techniques, like the 3 dimensional clay models, helped, but it didn't seem that his perspective was outside of himself. It actually seemed just the opposite. He was adept at thinking in a 3 dimensional manner, but his perspective seemed deep within himself. He became disoriented when dealing with too much outside stimulation. He also could read geometry and schematics just fine, understanding the concept of 3 dimensions while being able to see it in 2 dimensions.

Kyle needed to be officially and thoroughly tested. I felt enough was enough. We had to know what was really going on with him. I didn't want just someone's hour observation by one person. Kyle fell a little bit more behind every year despite my tutoring. The older he became, the more noticeable it was, and we had to do something. His grasp of mathematics was exceeding my own, and I didn't feel I would be able to help him with his homework much longer.

The year ended with our Kindergarten class "graduating". I was given hugs and sweet gifts from the students. One gift was a Bible from an Australian couple, in thanks for a Social Work assessment I had completed for their son. He went from being a "holy terror" to my "big helper". He was so bright and active. He just needed to be kept busy. I had tears in my eyes watching them leave that last day. I was so proud of all of them and I told them so.

Rick put in for a transfer, rather than ask for another tour. We got the news several months later: Rick was chosen to go to Minnesota rather than Seattle. We were scheduled to leave that September.

That September, I made a special trip to the lunch area to say goodbye to all my former Kindergarten students. I would miss them.

And then we headed to our new home: Minneapolis, Minnesota.

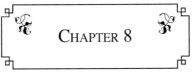

CHAPTER 8

Minnesota: Kyle is Autistic

We arrived in Minnesota that September, 2001. We all watched in horror as the world Trade Center collapsed due to a terrorist strike. I thought about all my Muslim friends at the International school and felt a deep sadness. We had often remarked over tea why it was that we could get along at the school and why couldn't the world do the same?

We enrolled Kyle and Caitlin in the Hopkins/Minnetonka school district. His teachers recommended that Kyle be assessed by a local panel of experts because they suspected that he had Asperger's syndrome. The panel would be made up of doctors, psychiatrists, social workers, clinical therapists and educators. The formal assessment would be comprehensive and somewhat lengthy. We agreed.

Several weeks later, after observation and testing, the panel agreed on a diagnosis.

Kyle was under the Autism Spectrum, not otherwise specified.

Autism! We were stunned. The doctors explained that Kyle understood humor and had compassion. He was expressive in relating to others, so he did not have Asperger's Syndrome. He did hyper-focus and transitions were stressful, but he could adjust, although he preferred a routine.

One doctor explained that he was high functioning. Another Doctor mumbled under his breath that Kyle wasn't THAT high functioning. I realized it was still all a matter of perception and opinion. While he fell under the Autism umbrella, Kyle was in a class all his own.

This was why the diagnosis was so difficult to pin down. I mumbled to Rick under my breath, "Well how high functioning does he have to be when he can do mathematics that I can't do?"

It all made sense: the rocking, the hyper-focusing, the organizing of his shoes and toys. It explained his fear of sudden, loud noises or movements, as well as his preference to rainy days and sunglasses to minimize the lights or the colors. It explained his sensitivity to touch, or the feel of certain clothing fabrics, and why he would eventually shut down if over stimulated. It also explained the lack of eye contact when he spoke to someone.

We were stunned now that we had the diagnosis. We worried. What would this mean for the rest of Kyle's life?

Could he marry and have a family?

Could he hold down a job?

Would people be unkind to him and discriminate against him forever?

And the most important question was, "How in God's name could we help him?"

Rick looked at me and said as we were driving home after receiving the news, "After all the quack diagnoses that we've gotten over the years, my faith in the Medical profession is destroyed. I think this diagnosis makes sense, but I'm never again going to believe hook, line and sinker what anyone says about Kyle–ever again. If Kyle can fish, he can work. Hell, he's a better fisherman than I am. If he can work, he can eat and provide for a family!" Rick rambled.

"And if he can provide for a family, he can marry. Why not? I want him to have a wife and children to love him, someday," I murmured.

"We're just going to have to be the ones to help him make it happen. I don't trust any of these so called experts anymore," Rick said grimly.

I nodded. I agreed with him.

"I don't know. Maybe–just maybe–they got it right this time and we go from here," Rick said tiredly as he looked out the window searching for something, anything.

I was still afraid.

I felt like an animal trapped in a cage. How to get out? How to help Kyle get out of this cage and live as "normal" a life as possible, or as full a life as he wanted to live, without the prejudice from other people?

The days passed and Kyle was put on an I.E.P, or an Individual Education Plan. The teachers and aides were extremely kind but Kyle came home frustrated day after day.

"Mom," Kyle said in exasperation one day. "They treat me like I'm an idiot now."

I nodded and chewed my lip.

Kyle was frustrated academically, while socially he needed help.

I got a call from one of his teachers one day. He told me that Kyle had given away all his lunch money to a boy. The boy gave him a sob story about being so poor, that Kyle bought him a pizza. He and his friends laughed at Kyle's gullibility. The teacher witnessed all this and had a talk with Kyle. I thanked him for telling me the story.

Kyle and I had a long talk when he got home from school. I wanted him to be generous. It was a hard lesson to learn that some people are actually drawn to this generosity and will take advantage selfishly.

Kyle came home a few days later and proudly stated that he had stood up to the boy. He refused to give him any more money. His teacher had coached him.

He was learning to make friends. He had befriended another special needs boy. They had begun playing a game called YU-GI-OH on the bus with other kids. The game was quite involved with summoning monsters to duel for you, and I was amazed that Kyle could play it so easily.

Kyle asked if his friend could spend the night and I said, "Absolutely!"

I was thrilled that Kyle had made a new friend.

I met the boy a few days later.

He seemed like a nice boy. It was also obvious that this boy had been pampered most of his life.

I watched them play together and realized two things. This boy used Kyle to do things for him that normally an aide would do, and this boy cursed like a sailor in order to get his way.

I was torn. I didn't feel that I could interfere, so I waited. And I waited.

The family went out for a hike around Lake Minnetonka one afternoon. Kyle began telling us about his friendship and asked us what we thought.

So, we voiced our opinions.

"Kyle, no one has the right to be disrespectful to you," I said. "I'm also concerned that he asks people to do some things for him that he could be learning to do for himself.

His parents do him a disservice because they won't live forever. The kindest thing would be to teach him independence," I cautioned.

"I'm not going to tell you who to be friends with, Bud, or who you can choose to be your friend," my husband said thoughtfully, carefully measuring his words. "Just make sure he really IS your friend. Friends don't call you names to get you to do things for them."

"I personally think he's taking advantage of you...he's kind of a jerk, Kyle," Cat chimed in and then frowned.

Kyle nodded and took it all in as we hiked through the beautiful Minnesota hiking trails along the lake. The trees were all turning gold, orange and reds for the Autumn Season, and we stopped to admire the geese sunning themselves by the tall grass.

Kyle ended the friendship some weeks later much to the boy's anger and dismay. I felt sorry for the boy, but I was relieved for Kyle's peace of mind. Kyle was more sensitive than anyone could know. No one ever imagines that a special needs child could be a bully, but I struggled watching Kyle come home feeling worthless. He was beaten down by the swearing and name calling. It was the right call for Kyle.

Kyle and I had some long discussions after that on the nature of friendships.

"Kyle, take this as a lesson. We need to start teaching you all those things that will help you live independently," I said one day. "I'm going to take these next few months to teach you. You're going to learn how to really clean, do laundry, cook, and buy groceries. I think this is a good idea. I'll give you an allowance for all your hard work. I'll give you more than most because I want you to save half of it for college."

"You really think I can go to college, Mom?" Kyle asked surprised.

"Yes, yes I DO!" I said convincing myself as well as Kyle. "I KNOW YOU CAN DO IT. We just have to find your niche, what you enjoy doing and what you do well. You're really good at fixing things and taking things apart. Remember, I had to beg you not to take my appliances apart?"

Kyle laughed.

"And how long did you keep your promise not to take apart the telescope?" I accused, cocking my eyebrow.

"Six months and no one would have known, except no one told me that those suckers are hermetically sealed. I did put it back together, but the telescope was shot at that point." Kyle laughed again, "Dad was pretty hot when he took it out to look at the full moon one night."

I shook my head with a smile. Kyle had to know how things worked. He would buy old T.V.s and radios just to take them apart.

Now, here was his passion.

The days passed sweetly. We cooked and laughed on the weekends. Kyle became a good cook, while Caitlin became a good baker. We experimented with new recipes. Kyle loved Middle Eastern cooking and Mexican. Caitlin loved Italian and East Indian food. The kids had house cleaning chores. We opened up bank accounts and showed them how to save half of their earnings. They seemed pleased as the accounts grew with each passing month. We talked about using their savings to go to college and the importance of education.

I was determined that Kyle would live a full, rich life. We went shopping and I taught them to look for bargains. We made it fun by finding cooking ingredients to different recipes we wanted to try. We went thrift shopping so I could show them the difference between resale and retail. We talked about quality vs. quantity and the craziness of buying fashions that all hinged on the status of "name brand". We even talked about quality and simplicity always being "in style". We dreamed and talked of their futures. We talked about all the possibilities that the world held for both of them.

Our home was a safe haven where we celebrated the seasons with food and fun, movies and games. Kyle had been bullied on the school bus until he became good at some of the games, YU-GI-OH in particular. Kyle took pride in winning the competitions and knowing all the rules involved in the game. He felt a real sense of accomplishment.

He even tried getting Cat to duel a couple of times. Cat is great at cards... regular cards. We play "Shanghai Rummy", "Kings in a Corner", and Rick taught her to play poker when she was six. She has quite the little poker face. YU-GI-OH was out of her league. YU-GI-OH is a game where there are rules, but they can change with each card played. She couldn't keep up. Their games usually ended with Cat throwing up her cards in disgust after losing. Kyle had studied for a while, and was unstoppable.

They had finished one game and Caitlin came to the kitchen while I cooked dinner one night.

"Are you letting him, win?" I asked skeptically while peering into her eyes.

"No, he's really good at this and I think the other kids are beginning to accept him now because he does win at these duels," Cat said as she reached for a cookie.

I mocked smacked the cookie from her hand.

"It's almost dinner time, you monkey." I pretended to be angry.

"You always say go for dessert first. You never know what's coming," Cat laughed.

"That's true...I do always say that. Keep it to one!" I laughed.

"So let me get this straight, this game is about summoning monsters, demons and gadgets to fight for you in an arena? Is that it?" I asked Cat.

"Yeah, it's all about strategy and you have to remember that different cards can change the rules at any time," she mumbled through her cookie.

I laughed at the crumbs spilling out of her mouth.

Kyle used strategy to change the rules to his own advantage while fighting demons and monsters.

I wondered.

Maybe this was the key to helping him in real life.

I watched him put away the game and I thought, maybe.

What if we used the rules to change the rules?

I felt a chill.

Kyle looked into the kitchen.

I smiled, really smiled for the first time in a long time.

CHAPTER 9

Chemo and Radiation

Kyle came to me a few weeks later. His arm ached. It was the same one he had broken several years before. I looked at it and said that I thought it was just growing pains. He was going through a growth spurt and puberty.

He came to me one week later and said, "Mom, this isn't growing pains. Look, this really hurts."

On his arm was a hard lump the size of a lemon. The lump hadn't been there the week before.

I took him to the doctor who referred me to a specialist. They took x-rays and ordered an M.R.I. We waited for the results.

The results came and we received a call to come in for a consultation.

We were shown pictures of a white mass–a cross section of his arm between the two bones: the radius and the ulna.

Kyle was diagnosed with a Desmoid Tumor. It was aggressive. It doubled in size within weeks and was the size of an orange. We were referred to an oncologist and a surgeon. The mass was scar tissue, technically, but was treated as a cancer because of its aggressive growth pattern.

The oncologist was extremely helpful and answered all our questions. She wanted Kyle to feel in control of his health care options. We were grateful to her for her sensitivity and respect. She recommended that we have a surgeon biopsy the mass to determine conclusively that it was a Desmoid Tumor, or another kind of tumor before treatment began.

"What is a Desmoid Tumor?" I asked.

She explained that a Desmoid Tumor was rare. Only 1 out of 3,000,000 are diagnosed with it. It is basically scar tissue that continues to grow aggressively invading the healthy tissues surrounding it. Kyle would need chemo-therapy or radiation if he had this condition.

We were referred to a surgeon. He came 45 minutes late. He didn't know our names. He hadn't read Kyle's file. He took one look at Kyle, and said that the arm had to be amputated.

"Kyle would like to try to save the arm, Doctor. What other options are available?" Rick asked.

He said the options were poor and that once he got into the operating room, no one would tell him how to operate.

"Doctor, I've read about some cutting edge surgeries where the surgeon goes into the tumor and cuts it up from the inside, removing the tumor internally," I countered.

He had never heard of the surgery.

We walked out fuming.

"Arrogant Jackass," Rick spat the words out in disgust.

"Ignorant Jackass. He was clueless," I countered.

We went back to the Oncologist and said that, as far as we were concerned, the surgeon was fired. "You can recommend any other surgeon, but not this one. I'm sure there are other competent surgeons that can perform the biopsy!" I said.

"Under no circumstance is this surgeon to perform any operation on our son!" Rick stated adamantly.

"Wow, that's not good," the oncologist countered. "What happened?"

We explained what happened. We concluded that we felt he was negative, rude and unwilling to work with us. The decision was Kyle's to make.

Kyle wanted to save his arm. So we spent the next six months trying first chemotherapy and then radiation. His chemo consisted of a "cocktail" of three different drugs. He had to report for the in-house chemo treatments in the Cancer Center at the University Medical school campus once a week for 3 months. Once the chemo was complete, they would reassess his prognosis.

Kyle was operated on to insert a "Port a Cath" in his upper chest. The device was hooked into an artery in his chest and acted as a "plug in" device for the chemo. The oncologist recommended it. She was afraid that, with the amount of chemo they were prescribing, he could form collapsed veins. Since the implant was considered "elective" surgery, it wasn't covered under our health plan. We went ahead with the surgery and it helped Kyle during the treatments.

I sat and cried watching Kyle hooked up to all the machines. He would puke into a yellow plastic bowl during the treatments.

I was so angry during this time. I had long, silent talks with God. "Enough already!" I would say angrily. "Isn't he burdened enough with the Autism? Please, God...give this kid a break," I would yell inside my mind while I looked up at the sky through the hospital windows.

I cried and I felt guilty. It seemed that Caitlin was always being pushed aside because Kyle needed so much attention.

I started picking Caitlin up from school for lunch once a

month. We would go to McDonalds for some special time, just the two of us. I began renting "girl" movies and once a week, we would spend time together. We would cuddle and watch romantic comedies which were her favorite. I hugged her often.

Rick's boss began giving him a hard time. He was coming in late so we could take Kyle to the hospital together.

"Can't your wife do it? Can't your wife take him to chemo?" he grumbled.

I shook my head when Rick told me.

"What, does FETCH AND CARRY appear on my fore-head? Do I LOOK like a Camp follower to you? What is wrong with this guy? Where is his compassion?" I shouted in exasperation.

My husband hugged me. "Look, I just told him: I'll come in late and I'll stay late. He'll get his money's worth out of me. What I don't get is that he's got kids of his own. How is it that he doesn't get this? I want to be there for my son."

Rick made every appointment, every one. Kyle noticed and when his treatments got rough, I would remind Kyle that his father came and never missed a chemo or radiation round.

"If you had to go through this Kyle, you couldn't be in a better place because we love you more than anything in the world. We'll make it through this somehow. Can you imagine going through something like this alone?" I said to Kyle one day. I just held his head on my shoulder. He seemed so weak and so sad, so TIRED.

He suffered so much during the chemo, that I began doubting my decision to try and save the arm. Maybe we should have let them take it.

The appointments were every week. The doctors would have Kyle sit in a large leather chair, and then they would plug in the I.V. bags of the chemo cocktail through the catheter in his chest. Kyle would vomit within minutes. Each session lasted two hours. We would take him back to school when it was over. We would stop at a vending machine on the way out and I would buy a Coke. I would beg Kyle to drink it after stirring the fizz out, so that the cola syrup would calm his stomach.

While we were waiting in the hallway during one of Kyle's procedures, a small 3 year old boy came out of a room across the hall.

He was hysterical.

"Please, Daddy, no. Don't make me do this. What did I do wrong? I'm sorry. I'll be good. I'll be good now. I promise, I promise. Please, Daddy, no," he pleaded and sobbed with his father who just shook his head with a look of defeat. The little boy was getting treatments, too.

I hid my head in Rick's shoulder and just sobbed. That little boy said everything that I had been thinking, and reflected everything I was feeling secretly.

"Why, God? Why? Please God, no. I promise we'll be good, we'll be better. Please God, NO!" I would imagine over and over.

Kyle lost weight. I tried making his favorite foods just to entice him to eat.

The Oncologist ordered a second M.R.I. to see how the tumor was affected by the chemo.

The results were grim. The chemo wasn't working. I looked over to Rick and saw the look of horror on his face. We discussed our options with the doctor.

Kyle's options were a de-bulking surgery where a surgeon goes in and attempts to cut out and remove as much of the tumor as possible. The second option was Radiation Therapy. Kyle's tumor was wrapped around the blood vessels and nerve bundles supplying the arm with oxygen as well as feeling. The de-bulking surgery could possibly damage and inhibit the use of his arm. The doctor recommended the radiation as the least invasive procedure. The risks, though, were possible cancers in the future. We discussed it as a family and asked Kyle what he wanted to do. He said without hesitation that he wanted to save the arm if possible and agreed to radiation.

Chemo ultimately didn't work and we regretted making him suffer. We were frustrated and exhausted. It was a terrible gamble either way.

Kyle began radiation and we agonized over the possible long term side effects. The radiation consisted of treatment five days a week, Monday through Friday. This lasted for six weeks at 45 minutes per treatment. He had the earliest appointment and then we would take him to school. Rick would drop me off at home and then he would head to work. These were grueling days.

We always let Kyle have the final say in his treatments. We felt it was important, since this was his whole life, despite the fact that he was only 13 years old. I wanted him to feel some sense of control over the process. I hoped it would help him heal.

It was at this time that I was determined to put away my smoking habit for good. I threw the cigarettes away in disgust, realizing that I couldn't encourage Kyle to make healthy food choices while "puffing away". The hypocrisy wasn't lost on me. I had to be strong for Kyle and this was one way I could do it.

I have often said, "If I could walk on water, I wouldn't be on this planet." It was humbling and I prayed to get through it. I began taking long walks to relieve my stress along the beautiful lakes in Minnesota. I would watch the wildlife along the lakes and feel calmer. I would watch the sun through the leaves. I'd feel the wind on my face trying to wake up and feel alive. I knew I had to be strong for Kyle. Who would hold him up until this was all over if I fell apart?

We came home after one particularly exhausting day. Kyle said he was going fishing. I thought it would help him. I secretly prayed that he would catch a fish.

Kyle came home an hour later with the biggest fish I had ever seen: a Northern Pike.

I took a picture and then called my husband.

"Kyle has the biggest fish I've ever seen swimming inside the bathtub," I laughed.

"No kidding! It's still alive after Kyle walked, what, a mile from the lake?" Rick sounded shocked.

"Yes, wait till you see this monster. I'll let you help him clean it tonight when you get home. I'm a little afraid of it," I giggled.

Rick came home and Kyle was excited to show him his catch. He led Rick upstairs.

"Hey, Bud, this is a Northern Pike and he's huge! I'm impressed," Rick said proudly.

"Yeah, he's a real monster. I caught it off the surface lure you gave me. He put up a huge fight," Kyle beamed.

Rick came downstairs and we smiled at each other. We were so grateful that Kyle had a real "win." Wins felt "few and far between" during that time of radiation treatments. Rick helped him clean the fish and cut open the stomach to look at the contents, which was their ritual. What they found in the stomach of this monster was a fully intact sunfish which he must have eaten just before being hooked. We ate Northern Pike that night after Kyle breaded and cooked it for us on the outdoor Hibachi. Rick let Kyle cook it with a few pointers on barbeque grilling. We all clapped and remarked at his wonderful skills as a fisherman. He proved that he would be able to provide for his family some day on his own. Kyle was thrilled.

"Kyle," Rick said as he looked at the trees in the back yard, "It's time we got you a real fishing pole. What do you say we go to Cabela's for your birthday and let you pick one out?"

Kyle's eyes widened. It was settled. This would be the big gift for his birthday. He was getting older and would often walk to the lake by himself to fish or to get away from the stress of school and medical treatments. The lake was his favorite place to think. He would now have a real fishing rod and his own tackle box.

We made arrangements the following week to go to Cabela's.

"Kyle, we're going to spend most of the day at this place. It's not a store, it's an experience," Rick laughed while driving.

Kyle smiled.

We arrived at Cabela's and spent most of the day there. We admired the giant aquarium that housed numerous species of fish. Kyle was mesmerized by the fish swimming. He and Rick scrutinized many fishing rods. They eventually settled on his favorite. We marveled at all the gadgets that were available for fishing.

We hiked a lot during that time period as a family. Minnesota has some of the most beautiful walking trails through woods and around lakes. There was a Wendy's at the end of one trail where we would usually buy one small milk shake and divide it into fours.

"Ice cream is always better shared," I used to say between bites and Caitlin always laughed. Money was really tight due to the increasing medical bills, so hiking was an inexpensive way for us to do something fun as a family. We had our best talks as a family on those hikes.

We decided to try out Kyle's new fishing rod after one of these hikes. While walking down to the lake, we came upon a snapping turtle on the trail. It was small–so small we thought it had just hatched and was trying to make it to the water. It got caught in the full sun and was going to die in the heat before reaching the water. One of its siblings had already died next to him.

"Look, it's a baby snapping turtle," Rick motioned to the ground.

"Aw, Mom, look at the turtle. He's trying so hard to make it to the lake. What will happen to him Dad?" Kyle said as his eyebrow furrowed.

"He'll probably be eaten by one of the fish. Very few turtles make it to maturity," Rick mused.

"Let's take him home and wait till he's bigger so he can survive," Kyle said excitedly.

So, Rick found an old paper cup and used it to scoop up the turtle. Kyle put some water in the cup to cool off the turtle.

They placed the turtle in an old aquarium and took it to Kyle's room. The turtle thrived under Kyle's care. He hand fed this turtle fish/turtle food. He put rocks and a small dish for a makeshift pond and dirt. I imagined it was quite cozy for a turtle. Soon, he was eating strips of fish from Kyle's hand.

"You're going to be a wonderful father, someday," I said while watching him feed his turtle from the doorway of his room.

"You know, Mom, he's never bitten me," Kyle said thoughtfully. "Not even once."

I smiled. "I mean it. You're very loving and gentle. You're going to be a real blessing to your children," I said giving him a hug.

I said these things to encourage myself as much as Kyle. I was hanging on to a future thread of hope. I emotionally thought that if I meditated on it enough, we could make it happen.

Was I hopelessly looking through rose colored glasses?

It was a hope borne from desperation. There was nothing to do but hope. The alternative was empty and unthinkable.

"We have to hang in there Rick," I whispered to him one day. "If we lose it, then who will be there for Kyle? We're it!"

Rick nodded. He seemed to age overnight watching Kyle suffer.

During this time, when Kyle was suffering, my cousins were my best friends. They called often, sometimes daily. They offered to pray for us. They offered to ask their churches to pray for us. My cousin Susan sent anointed prayer cloths to tuck under Kyle's pillow. My cousin Tina made me see the funny side of things, having watched a loved one go through chemo. They laughed with me, they let me cry. I don't know how I would have made it through that time without the support of my cousins.

I found myself telling Kyle that we had to eat healthier. We went organic. The doctors thought that all the hormones and chemicals in un-organic foods may have contributed to tumor growth. We started to eat only organic foods. We avoided certain foods high in sugar or fat. Certain dairy products like cheese or nuts were to be avoided. Kyle could eat these in moderation, so we added them as a condiment only.

After the sixth week, another M.R.I. was ordered to see if the radiation was having any effect on the tumor. We waited for the results.

One day, while we were waiting, I opened the sliding glass door to let our collie "Chino" outside. As I opened the door, an enormous snake slid right into the house over my foot.

I screamed and ran for the telephone.

"Rick, Rick, a huge black snake ran into the house. What do I do?" I felt the panic rising in me. I remembered all the stories about copperheads and water moccasins from my childhood in Michigan.

"Well, take a look at it and see if the eyes are round or slit," Rick said in exasperation.

"ARE YOU CRAZY? I'm not getting that close to see what kind of eyes it has," I screamed back, imagining fangs bared coming at my face.

Just then Kyle said, "Aw, Mom, he's just as afraid of you. Look"

I turned around and Kyle had the snake perched on a snake hook an inch away from my face.

I heard myself scream and dropped the phone.

"Get that thing away from me, oh my God, put it down, NO! Don't put it down. Wait….I." I picked up the phone. "Rick, I'll call you back."

"Look, Mom, isn't that cute? He's pretending to be dead," Kyle pointed to the snake that was now completely limp with its mouth hanging open.

"Kyle, honey. Do you think you could carefully, CARE-FULLY, put that outside?" I asked tentatively.

"Can we keep it?" Kyle asked wide eyed.

"No, Honey, just put it outside, CAREFULLY…yep, carefully" I smiled nervously.

Kyle sighed, "Oh. Okay, Come on little guy."

And just like that, Kyle took the snake outside and gently put his two fingers behind the snake's head. He placed the snake on the ground and quickly let go. The snake was still playing dead but a few minutes later, the snake was gone, having slithered into the tall grass.

I was in awe of my son. That took real skill!

"Promise me, Kyle, you won't bring anything home that's poisonous, okay?" I bargained with him later that night as he was telling the story to Rick. They both smiled as they continued to talk about snakes and catching them.

A few days later, the results of the MRI were complete and we got the call to come in.

We met with the doctor to go over the results and saw her smile.

There were no signs of the tumor visible in the M.R.I. The radiation had knocked the tumor down and killed it. We were all ecstatic.

We all cried with gratitude. We thanked all the doctors who had worked so hard on Kyle's behalf. We were so happy for Kyle. The tumor continued to shrink until it was an ever present, unspoken memory. Kyle was told to have a follow up M.R.I every six months for one year and then one every year thereafter. If the tumor was gone for five years, they would declare him cured and "cancer" free.

A few weeks after the good news, we were in the grocery store. Kyle recognized one of the Oncology nurses who said hello to him.

He immediately puked.

"I'm so sorry," Kyle said miserably. He was embarrassed.

"This happens all the time when I see one of my patients," she said kindly with a sad smile.

"I hope you don't take it personally," I winced realizing that she didn't.

Then, the medical bills came.

We shook our heads in disbelief.

The chemo was $800 dollars per treatment. We had saved almost fifty thousand dollars in bonds for the kids' education, and had some I.R.A's. We cashed all the bonds and most of the I.R.A's. It still wasn't enough by half to cover what the insurance companies did not cover. We established a payment plan.

We ate a lot of homemade soup that year. Our Christmas tree was filled with necessities that both kids needed for school, and most of it came from thrifts shops or garage sales. We celebrated with homemade treats and were thankful for them.

And we were grateful, maybe because we took nothing for granted. We cherished each other and our health. We cherished what beautiful things we had, and didn't worry about the things we didn't have. We didn't have the energy to do anything else. Nothing was as important as Kyle's life.

We continued hiking again as a family. Some times, when we ended up at Wendy's on a pay day, we would splurge between the four of us and add a one dollar burger to the small milkshake. We would laugh as we cut it into fours and shared it. It was all we could afford, but we enjoyed it and felt blessed we could afford even that. I will admit, we sometimes scoured the sofa cushions and purses to come up with the change to pay for even that.

We were slowly paying our bills and we still had a roof over our head. We were lucky and we knew it.

I still paid the kids an allowance. It was the only money that they had for school activities and fun with their friends.

We stopped by Kyle's school that winter to pick Kyle up one day. The principal yelled from across the room, "Hey, Kyle, Chanukahs coming up isn't it?"

Kyle yelled back, "I dunno...maybe."

We all laughed at his assumption that we were Jewish.

I told the kids later, "God has a sense of humor. I'm Catholic, your father is Protestant, I was raised in a Muslim country, you were raised in a Buddhist country and we have a Jewish last name. I think that wraps it up."

None of these differences meant anything to me. They seemed pointless in the face of real human suffering, and equally pointless in the sharing of real human joy. No philosophy was ever more important to me than one single smile from a child, or one single act of human kindness shared. It seemed to me that religious ideology only served to keep us isolated from other people. I sometimes wondered if ideology and ritualized rules kept us from feeling closer to God, as well.

Although, with all my flaws, I didn't really need any help in that area! I was in constant prayer at that time asking God for guidance and understanding in all that we had been through as a family. I've often said that I'm not necessarily a good person. The difference is that I WANT to be a good person. I'm just a person who's willing–willing to let God guide me one moment at a time. It's humbling, frustrating and exasperating trying to put yourself, your own will aside. I'm not always successful, much like meditation. Put aside ME, ME, ME and bring yourself gently back with one thought: compassion. Of course, this only works if you're compassionate with yourself as well as others and it's easier said than done.

Caitlin came home that spring concerned about one of her friends. Her friend's mother was really broke, a single mother struggling to make ends meet. She couldn't afford day care for both her children.

I had a brilliant idea.

I discussed it with Kyle.

"What do you think about babysitting a 7 year old boy? If you do a good job, you might get a letter of recommendation which could lead to other jobs. I could be on hand to supervise, although I'd make you do it. You'd have to really be responsible for his safety. You'd have to cook dinner and clean up the apartment. Sometimes you could dust and vacuum the house before she came home," I said excitedly.

"I know how to do all those things," Kyle said thoughtfully.

"When I was a child, my favorite babysitter was the boy who lived next door. He was really good to us and kind. We loved him. There's no harm in a boy babysitting. It's a good job, but it's a huge commitment. You'd be giving up your whole summer. Are you prepared to do that? Once you give his mother your word, you have to keep your word," I counseled.

Kyle thought about it for a minute and then agreed. He had been eyeing an Xbox to play video games, and that was something we just couldn't afford. We discussed the fact that if he saved half of his pay, he would still have enough to buy the machine.

He agreed wholeheartedly.

I called the boy's mother and explained our plan. I said that her daughter could hang out at our house for free with my daughter as well. Kyle would charge her half to watch her little boy than what the day care would cost for the entire summer.

She agreed. I was grateful for this wonderful opportunity for Kyle. Several of his teachers wrote letters of recommendation for the job. They praised his responsibility and hard work ethic.

Kyle spent the summer babysitting this little boy. It was one of the best summers of Kyle's life, and his mother later claimed her son loved Kyle. Kyle took him for bike rides and took him fishing. They went for hikes and played games. They watched movies or played video games. They divided their time between the houses. Kyle always went back to the little boy's home in time to make dinner and straighten up the house.

This woman gladly wrote Kyle a letter of recommendation at the end of the summer. Kyle wondered at all the money he had earned. He put half of his summer earnings in his savings account for college, and then bought the Xbox as his reward. He felt such a sense of pride and accomplishment.

"I liked having a job, Mom," Kyle said.

"And you liked having your own money to spend the way you wanted, too!" I laughed.

"Yeah, I really do." Kyle smiled.

"This is really going to help you get another job someday, Kyle. You'll see." I nodded.

It was one of the most rewarding summers of Kyle's life

CHAPTER 10

Colorado

That summer gave Kyle confidence in doing a job well. It also gave him an appreciation for work as an opportunity to make money, not as a necessary evil, but as a privilege. He was lucky to have the work and it allowed him to do some fun things, and buy some fun things. He seemed sure of himself and more in control of his emotions. He seemed calmer, too.

I was so proud of him.

We left at the end of that summer because Rick retired. He wanted more time with the kids, and his heart surgeries impressed upon him the importance of making everyday matter.

I had done an online search looking at several places to retire. I called a small town in Washington State near the Canadian border where we had property. All the special needs kids were bussed an hour away to a larger town.

I called a small town in Montana. The principal couldn't have been friendlier. He explained that his school did have a special needs program: the kids were given a broom and taught how to sweep the gymnasium floor. I thought he was kidding and waited for the rest. There was an awkward silence as I realized this was the entire program and there was no punch line, this was no joke. I thanked him for his time. I hung up the phone and bugged my eyes out while mouthing a silent WHAT!

I finally called the High School in a small town in the Colorado Rocky Mountains. Yes, they had a special needs program. I was actually impressed with the comprehensive nature of the special needs program. They worked up I E P's or Individual Education Plans, meeting the unique needs of the individual child. For some children pushing a broom was appropriate, for other children the tasks were more advanced. They had group classes for special needs but also emphasized mainstreaming as much as possible. The progress of each student was assessed quarterly.

We decided to move back to Colorado. Rick was a "military brat" and Colorado was the only place he ever considered home. He had moved around often as a child, but when his father was stationed as an Air Force Colonel in Colorado, they were able to stay in one place for a few years. During his high school years, he spent a lot more time with his father. They hiked and fished together often. His mother had a garden and he learned how to grow vegetables. He learned to bow hunt and shoot. He felt Colorado was a sportsman's paradise.

Rick's mother still lived in Colorado. We could be closer to his mother and give both children a sense of extended family. He was committed to the idea of putting down roots so that both kids could go to one High School without moving again. Rick had moved so much growing up that he always felt like the new kid who never fit in. He became a loner. He excelled at all the things a person could do alone: running, shooting, hiking and camping. He was determined that our children would have more of a sense of community and make friends before their senior year.

I agreed. I moved around constantly as a child myself and always felt like the new kid too. I'm strong willed (too much so sometimes) and I'm kind when people approach me. What people don't understand is that I'm actually shy by nature. I agonize over social exchanges with an anxiety I keep hidden from most people. I do this by always encouraging others to talk about themselves. I "refuel" by being alone: reading, writing, contemplation, prayer, rather than being in group situations. I've learned that many kids who grow up in the military or government services become "learned extroverts" to compensate for the constant readjustments in their environments. It makes children independent, but we wanted our children to have some sense of stability, even if only for a short time.

I was hopeful that the school was the right fit for Kyle. I also wanted them to get to know their Grandmother better and spend time with her. Our children were in a sense "Government Brats", and while moving to so many places helped them adjust quickly to new situations, I wanted them to have a sense of being grounded. I wanted them to experience life in "small town America" where people still knew their neighbors. We also discussed the fact that it was important for the children to see us helping Rick's mom. Rick's dad had passed away a few years prior, and Rick wanted to be in a position to help her. We wanted to show Kyle and Caitlin that it is a privilege and an honor to care for one's aging parents. We felt this was one of the greatest lessons we could teach them: As we care for our parents, so will you care for us someday. This is our greatest gift to you because someday your children will see this and, if you're fortunate, will care for you in the same way when your time comes.

This, sometimes, annoyed Rick's mother. She is extremely independent and was climbing Pikes Peak during this time. Pikes Peak is a "fourteener" or over 14,000 feet in elevation. Needless to say, she was in better shape then we were and this had some comical, if unintended outcomes, as we struggled to keep up with her during hikes. Still, we wanted to show Kyle and Caitlin that being there for your family was important: sharing holidays and school functions, triumphs and challenges.

I did an online search for homes in Colorado. The prices were grim and I just didn't know how we were going to afford Colorado home prices. We got a lucky break when we found a buyer for our property in Washington. So, I found a few affordable homes for Rick to look at when he went to Colorado.

Affordable!

That's right: Cheap.

We had bought a painting when we were first married. It was a mountain scene with two trees on either side of the mountain and a lake to the right just under the mountain. We had always joked that we wanted to live in that painting someday. Rick hated every house on my list as he toured one by one with the realtor. Rick has Champagne tastes and will buy only the very best. I shop at thrift stores and buy affordable bargains. Needless to say, my idea of affordability was a "fixer" and that's what I had flagged. As he was shown the last house on the list, he just shook his head in disgust even though the house was on a lake. He was ready to give up when they passed by a cedar home that had

just come on the market and wasn't listed yet. Rick asked
the Realtor to stop the car.

"What about this one?" Rick said. "Can we see this one?"
The Realtor said she'd make a few calls. She was successful and they made an appointment for that afternoon.

Rick walked up to the front door later that day and, as
he turned to look beyond the deck, there was the painting
in every detail: a mountain above a lake with blonde grass
and trees on either side of it. Even the trees were the same:
Aspen and Pine. It was the place we had always wanted to
live. He said he got chills when he saw it for the first time.

He called me an hour later and excitedly told me about
the house. He described the house and the cost. Could we
afford it?

Now, as I said, I'm the bargain hunter. I had lined up
houses I felt we could afford...which meant dogs that had
potential with a little elbow grease. This house was beautiful by the sound of it. Rick always had impeccable taste.
I told him to go ahead and put an offer on the house since
I suspected it wouldn't stay on the market for long. I
asked Rick to send me pictures of the house.

That's right.

We bought a house that I had never seen. My horrified
friends thought this was madness, but I took a step in faith.
We were going home. I did the math and called him back.

"We can afford this house if we eat a lot of soup," I said.

"I like soup," he replied sheepishly.

I knew then he really wanted this house. He was excited
and the pictures were grand.

We packed up the house. Caitlin said tearful goodbyes to
all her friends. She had made many of them. She wanted

to stay: coffee shops, Mall of America, skating rinks and movie theatres. I called her my social Butterfly, while Rick laughingly called her his Mall rat.

"Colorado isn't at the end of the world," I said as I hugged her reassuringly. "You'll make friends there just like you did here in Minnesota."

We drove cross country. Several days later, we arrived in Colorado and headed up the mountain to our new home.

Now, I was born in the ghetto of Detroit. My dad was a Detroit Police officer and, in the days of my childhood, Cops were expected to live within the city limits of their precincts. That's right–a Motown city girl. As we drove for miles and miles without a soul in sight, I began to get nervous.

"This is a good place to bury a body, honey. Where are all the people, the neighbors?" I asked for reassurance.

Caitlin turned her nose up in disgust.

"This place isn't even civilized! There are no malls, there isn't even a Starbucks. We gave up Mall of America for this?" she raged. From the back seat of the car I heard Cat singing the theme song to the show "Green Acres".

Cat sang the entire song with a sneer.

"Will you knock it off? " I said as I scowled at her.

We finally pulled into the housing development and I saw a few neighbors. I breathed a sigh of relief.

And then I saw the house.

Rick sheepishly waited for my reaction.

I just stood and stared at the mountain for a few minutes, trying to take it all in.

It was beautiful and it was our painting. I couldn't believe it. It was as if we were meant to be in this place. It had a view of the mountains and a small lake. We were in the middle of

the woods. I felt we had an angel over our shoulders. I looked at all this to the tune of "Green Acres." I sighed and smiled.
I felt that we had at last come home.

KYLE IS A HEALTHY BABY

KYLE'S FAVORITE TOY - A DUCK THAT
QUACKED WHEN WALKED

KYLE IS WEARING HIS FATHER'S
F4 FIGHTER HELMET

ONE OF THE AIR SHOWS WE ATTENDED

RICK DURING HIS TOUR OF DUTY

Halloween

Kyle visits the Elephant Farm

KYLE AND CAT FISHING ON
THE COLUMBIA RIVER

KYLE IN MINNESOTA WHEN HE WAS
DIAGNOSED AS AUTISTIC

KYLE ON PROM DAY

KYLE THANKS THE MAYOR FOR THE CITIZEN OF
THE QUARTER AWARD.

KYLE WAS NOMINATED BY MEMBERS OF THE HIGH SCHOOL FACULTY.
HE WAS SECRETLY TUTORING SPECIAL NEEDS STUDENTS AFTER
MAINSTREAMING INTO REGULAR CLASSES.

WE COULDN'T BE MORE PROUD OF HIM!

KYLES'S HIGH SCHOOL GRADUATION DAY
WITH CAT AND MOM

CYNDERS, THE CAT

KYLE RAISES HIS NEW STUB TO SAY "STUBS RULE."
HE ATTENDED CAT'S BALLROOM DANCE COMPETITION
ABOUT SEVEN WEEKS AFTER HIS AMPUTATION.

KYLE, RANGER AMANDA AND CAT

Kyle today outside of Boeing,
where he is employed as a Quality Control
Specialist / Airplane Mechanic Inspector.

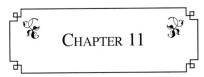

CHAPTER 11

Special Needs and Discrimination in High School

COLORADO

We spent a few days settling into the new house and unpacked. We enrolled the kids into the new schools. Kyle would start High School and Caitlin was in her last year of Middle School.

We were putting the house in order when I looked downstairs and noticed Kyle hadn't cleaned his room, or put away his things. I realized he was upstairs playing on the computer.

I yelled upstairs.

"Kyle, YOU COME DOWN HERE RIGHT NOW AND CLEAN YOUR ROOM. I MEAN IT KYLE. I WILL GROUND YOU."

Kyle replied without missing a beat, "Kyle's not home right now, but if you leave your name, number and the time you called, he will get back to you. BEEEEEP!"

There was a moment of silence.

And then, I lost it. I started laughing and I couldn't stop.

I tried to tell him to clean his room again and stopped midway breathless from the laugher.

I could hear him laughing upstairs too.

"Okay, you have a reprieve: one day. I mean it Kyle," I laughed.

"Okay, Mom," Kyle laughed back.

I met several of the teachers in the Special Needs program later that week when Kyle started school. They seemed supportive, but skeptical of all the things Kyle had accomplished. They repeatedly underestimated what he could do. I explained that he could clean, cook, grocery shop. They smiled dubiously as they read over his paperwork, in that guarded, absentminded way. The aides, on the other hand, couldn't have been more helpful. They were sensitive and really worked hard on behalf of the students.

I got several calls over the next few months. One of the teachers said Kyle had rage issues and lacked direction. One teacher said he was acting out and gave me literature on possible group homes for the future. This same teacher confided in me that his real love was coaching (any sport), and he had only entered into the Special Needs program for job security. I was surprised at this admission, although Rick wasn't.

"People tell YOU the strangest things," Rick would say and shake his head in amazement.

I felt unnerved by the admission, though, and secretly wondered what kind of help Kyle would receive under his care. I was determined to keep an even closer eye on Kyle's education.

Kyle was frustrated. He rode to school on the "Short Bus" for the Special Needs kids. The bus drivers loved him because he was polite and helpful, but riding the bus marked him.

One day, Caitlin came home really angry. A kid on the

regular bus had asked her who rode the "Retard Bus."

She told him, "Shut up, my brother rides that bus."

It was always there, this stigma.

I would watch him standing alone after the regular bus left with Cat and her friends.

One day, while he was waiting alone, a black cat from across the street ran playfully over to Kyle. He jumped up on two legs, stretched his paw up onto Kyle's chest as if to say, "Hey!"

Kyle laughed and petted him. The cat sat down and waited with Kyle until the bus came. I could see Kyle looking down at the cat periodically while they waited. He smiled in appreciation. Once the bus had left, the cat ran back to his home.

I marveled at that cat and said a silent prayer of thanksgiving. It seemed like that cat was just the thing that Kyle needed: an unexpected friend.

That cat came everyday. Shadow was his name. He belonged to the girls who lived across the street. He would run with them to the bus and wait until they got on. Then he would run back, turn and see Kyle standing there. He always ran back and sat next to Kyle until he boarded his own bus.

I marveled at this as I drank my coffee in the morning.

I loved that cat and took his little company as an angel from God.

Ironically, the "short bus" was as much a refuge as a stigma for Kyle, and he was popular on the Special Needs bus. He often laughed about the playful antics of the bus driver, the kindness of the aide and how he helped the other kids who needed help. He liked the idea of helping the other kids off the bus at the end of the ride. The appreciative nods from the bus driver made him smile. It made him feel strong and useful.

And then one day this changed.

Kyle came home after school absolutely crushed.

"What's wrong?" I asked alarmed.

"Mom, I read my file today. The teacher left it on the desk and I read it while he was at lunch," He said quietly.

"Uh oh," I thought. "No good ever comes from reading a secret file. Here we go."

Kyle had tears running down his face.

"Mom, the teacher said that I was operating on a third grade level."

Then Kyle handed me some literature that recommended he become a "Super Senior" and stay in High School an extra 2 years.

I looked at the literature. I felt a coldness that went beyond rage.

I was also frightened. I felt that this program would actually flag Kyle as a "problem" and keep him from getting a job in the future. I truly believed work, that Kyle felt passionate about, would be his salvation.

One of the teachers who sent the literature home sincerely believed that being a Super Senior was the only way for Kyle to get the "help" he needed. I chose to believe that her intentions were heartfelt, but I knew that Kyle could do so much more.

I suspected, too, that the program needed students to continue the funding for the program.

I also sensed that, when Kyle deviated from the norm of a particular program, he was labeled as a "problem" despite the fact that he was supposed to be on his OWN program.

I had worked in a group home for a few months. The group home I had seen was a home shared by 3-4 people. Each resident has their own room that is specific to their physical or mental needs. They usually share a common bathroom and common kitchen. Each house has a care provider who helps with bill paying, cleaning, shopping and cooking. The care provider also arranges for transportation or drives the residents in a house van. They were wonderful places for the truly incapacitated, but Kyle was so intelligent that I felt it would crush his spirit. I had found that it was often difficult for people in group homes to find work or people willing to let them work. Sometimes these houses, instead of truly helping the residents become independent, enabled them to languish in a strange self-styled dependency. The care provider "worked" for the resident who enjoyed a sense of contemptuous control and entitlement.

I muttered under my breath while shaking my head, "Not on my watch."

I sat Kyle down.

"Kyle, listen to me very carefully. I know that you're smart, but you're so angry that other people can't see it. Kyle you're so smart that you're the kind of kid who could fall through the cracks. You won't qualify for public assistance in the future. I guarantee it, honey. If you don't pull yourself together, you could end up homeless someday. Kyle you have to be MORE polite, MORE hardworking, MORE clean-showered and groomed than the other guy. I have always told you that your Autism wasn't going to be an excuse to be lazy, disrespectful or dirty," I counseled.

He remained silent.

"Kyle, look at me," I said as I pointed two fingers at my

eyes like I used to do when he was small. He continued to look down at his hands. He was nervously fisting and releasing his fingers.

"You think I'm going to be homeless," Kyle said resentfully.

"Look at me."

He did.

I said, "If you don't get serious and focus on making your life what you want it to be, you could end up homeless, yes, on the streets. There are no real programs for someone with your intelligence. That's what I said." I searched his eyes for some recognition of my words.

"I promise you that you're going to have a good job, your own home and a loving family some day. I'll move Heaven and Earth to help you. I know you can do this. Don't let this man or anyone else tell you, WHO YOU ARE, OR WHAT YOU'RE WORTH!" I said with a grim forcefulness.

"Mom, I swear that I'm going to show him that he's wrong. I am smart. I'm going to show him," Kyle said, wiping the tears from his face.

I hugged him and nodded, "We'll show him, Baby. You'll see."

Weeks passed and Kyle still seemed very angry and sullen. I was wracking my brain trying to find ways to reach him and encourage him. I felt it was essential that Kyle have a spiritual life to tap into in times of stress. Prayer was crucial, but how could I encourage him to do it? We were more spiritual than religious as a family. We always encouraged the kids to respect religious diversity in other cultures. Still, I had been raised Catholic. I did have faith that there was some design, some meaning to these struggles in life.

144

I had to believe that God cared. There had to be some purpose to this struggle. There had to be some meaning of hope for Kyle as well as others on the other side of all this suffering.

When I was a child, one of my relatives suffered from a condition called 'Pigeon' toes. She had to wear heavy black shoes that slowly corrected her walk. The shoes were painful and ugly. She would beg her mother not to put them on her feet. But, every day her mother would cry as she put those shoes on her feet. She knew that without them, the child would be crippled for life. In order to walk, she had to wear the shoes for at least a little while.

I was telling Kyle this story as we were driving on the road early one winter morning after a doctor's appointment. I looked around and there was no one else on the road.

"Maybe that's how it is for us. Maybe the struggles that we suffer are like those shoes. The struggle heals us and keeps us from being crippled spiritually so we can walk the right way," I mused.

"Kyle," I asked, "I've raised you to believe in God, and Jesus with his message of love and compassion as our salvation. Between me and you, what do you really believe?"

I looked out the window, not a soul in sight on this winter morning.

Kyle seemed surprised. "Well, Mom....I believe in God, but I'm not sure I believe he's all powerful. It's easier for me to believe what I can see or feel in the real world"

"Wow," I said stunned. "What would God have to do to show you He's all powerful, and that he cares about you, and listens to your prayers?"

"Mom," said Kyle sarcastically, "He'd have to make

a snake appear right here, right now in the middle of the highway for me to believe."

I remember feeling the prayer as I looked up to the winter sky rather than saying the words, "Ok, Lord, it's up to you. I truly have faith that you're listening. Please encourage him. If ever anyone needed to be close to you for guidance, ITS KYLE!"

Just at that moment, a car came out of nowhere, and zoomed past us. "Wow," Kyle said surprised," You don't see those every day."

"Why, what is it?" I was confused.

"That's a Dodge Viper," Kyle said with admiration.

I was silent for a moment, stunned.

"A Viper. You mean a snake?" I said cocking my eyebrows.

"What?" Kyle said with a look of slowly mounting horror on his face.

"You told God it had to be a snake, Kyle; you didn't say it had to be a REAL snake. You just said snake," I said smiling while pointing a finger at his chest.

It began to dawn on Kyle just what had happened.

We both started to laugh nervously.

"Oh my God, Oh my GOD," Kyle repeated over and over.

I started to laugh and couldn't stop.

Yep, God has a sense of humor.

From that moment on, whenever Kyle got discouraged, I always reminded him of the Dodge Viper. I used that story over and over to encourage Kyle to pray. I encouraged him to ask God for help with his problems and for guidance in making decisions. I was secretly grateful and prayed, myself, that God would help him with his anger.

Still, Kyle seemed lost, despite my encouragement to pray. He couldn't see beyond the daily frustrations and rejections he faced. His anger was actually keeping him stuck in a world of resentment and suspicion. The rage was always just below the surface for him.

One day he came to me.

"Mom, I just feel discouraged because there are so many things that the teachers tell me I can't do," Kyle fumed.

"Kyle, don't concentrate on what you CAN'T do, just focus on what you CAN do and go from there. What do YOU want to do with your life?" I said while making supper.

"I dunno," he whispered.

"Okay, look you know God listens to your prayers because he gave you a Viper," I laughed.

Kyle smirked and shook his head as if he regretted ever making that challenge.

"I want you to pray tonight before you go to bed and ask God for a dream. Ask God what you should do with your life! You just have to have faith when you ask for the dream," I cautioned.

"Okay, Mom, but I don't remember my dreams," Kyle shrugged.

"That's okay; you can ask God to REMEMBER too," I said, giving Kyle a sample of the spaghetti sauce to taste.

So, that night he prayed.

The next day: Nothing.

He prayed again the next day: Nothing.

On the third day, he woke up and joined me for coffee.

"Mom, I had a weird dream this morning just before I woke up," Kyle said sleepily.

"Yeah?" I mumbled yawning into my coffee.

"I dreamt that I was standing in front of a Boeing 747 Airplane," Kyle said surprised.

As he said it, I saw in my mind the same picture only Kyle had a wrench in his hand.

"Wow that seems pretty clear. Okay! That's good enough for me!" I said as my eyes widened.

Okay God, here goes.

We had been taking Kyle to air shows all his life. He loved mechanics. He loved airplanes and engines. It just never occurred to me that he would become an airplane mechanic. I don't know why. It should have been obvious.

I spent the next few days looking for airplane mechanic schools across the country. I found one north of Denver which was the closest one to us: Redstone College.

I called and asked if I could speak to someone about touring the facility over the summer. The woman on the phone explained that since Kyle was only a sophomore, it was unusual but we could join the summer orientation for a tour.

I thanked her profusely. I was excited about the prospect of showing Kyle an actual college. I was hoping it would encourage him to focus on a goal if he could actually see and feel the facility.

We drove up a few weeks later and joined the Freshmen Orientation.

From the moment we arrived, Kyle was in awe of the planes and the engines. We toured the facility and Kyle asked questions about the different programs available: Airframe and Power-plant was the study for airplane mechanics. This was the program Kyle was most excited about because he was fascinated by the engines.

When I finished the tour, I realized the school was ideal because Redstone was a relatively small college. The instruction was primarily "hands on" which was the best way Kyle learned. I thought that Kyle would do well with the emphasis on doing rather than reading.

On the way home, I listened to Kyle excitedly talk about the program. He talked and talked. I had never seen him so psyched. I smiled and nodded.

WE HAD A GOAL.

Over the next few weeks that summer, we talked about Kyle going to the college. We went over the steps he needed to take to make this dream happen.

We agreed that Kyle would have to take as many science and math courses as he could including Calculus, Physics, and Chemistry. I eventually got him some books "courses for dummies" on all these subjects. I encouraged him to read them on his own over the summer before taking the classes, just like we did when he was a child. He would have to fight to take some of these courses since he was in the Special Needs program. I also wondered out loud if it wouldn't be better to wean him out of the Special Needs program. It was a sanctuary in some ways, but it wouldn't prepare him for the future he was trying to create.

Rick had some doubts since we both struggled in math, but I assured him that Kyle wasn't like us. He was GOOD in math.

Kyle decided that he would work really hard to get out of the Special Needs program by his senior year of High School. That would give him 2 years to mainstream, and then he could apply to the College. Since the college was a technical college/Associates degree, the emphasis would not be on Reading/English which were Kyle's most challenging subjects.

"What about the Special Ed teachers, Mom?" Kyle said chewing his lip in thought.

"Just think of them as speed bumps. You have to slowly get past them. Just be determined. Come hell or high water, you're going to Redstone College. We just have to plan carefully. You need to mainstream, take the math courses to qualify for the college. You'll need to get a drivers license. A job would be helpful, too," I rambled as my mind raced on fast forward.

I thought for a moment forcing myself to slow down to look at the steps.

"Lets just take it one step at a time, okay? You'll have Drivers Ed with "Coach". Dad and I have already paid the fee for him to teach you. He says despite the fact that you're in Special Ed, he says you have the eye/hand coordination to learn. He has confidence in you. He told me so," I said with a smile.

"Really?" Kyle said surprised.

"Listen, Kyle, there's no pressure here. Just learn to drive. If you have to take the course more than once, then so be it. Who cares? As long as you eventually pass and get that license, that's all that matters," I said defiantly.

Kyle nodded, "I'm going to show them, Mom, I'm going to."

That school year, Kyle and Caitlin both took lessons after school. Coach was an amazing man who encouraged Kyle and instilled confidence in him.

Of course, the first day, Kyle began joking, "We're all going to die!" when Caitlin took the wheel. Not amused,

Coach threatened to leave him on the side of the road. Kyle kept his apocalyptic thoughts to himself after that when Caitlin was driving. Coach's enthusiasm was contagious, and that lead to both Kyle and Cat completing the course successfully. The entire plan hinged on Kyle getting that driver's license from DMV. If he could do that, then everything else would follow. He could get a job and get experience working with others. This would better prepare him for the transition to working with others in college.

Once they got through the course, then it was up to us, as parents, to drive with them over a year's time period. They needed so many hours of daytime/nighttime driving. Coach could administer the DMV test himself in town after the driving hours were completed. I felt so grateful. I also felt that if Coach could administer the test, having taught him, Kyle would be more relaxed and succeed. If we could avoid one of the examiners at the DMV where it was crowded, confusing, and busy then it would be easier on Kyle. If he could successfully drive with his under 21 license without accident, then the DMV would have to give him a license despite his being different.

I drove with Kyle and Rick drove with Caitlin. We agreed to divide and conquer. Rick was constantly breaking an imaginary break pedal on the passenger's side of the car when he drove with Kyle. I did too, but less often. Kyle seemed to respond to my quiet voice compared to Rick's screaming. My first day with Caitlin, I found myself screaming for her to stop before we drove into a ditch.

"Mom, you're scaring me," She fumed.

"I'M SCARING YOU?" I yelled back.

I'm a nervous driver. When I was a Federal Agent in my twenties, I survived a couple of high speed chases. You know–the kind of car chases where the car is on two wheels going 100 mph on a raised overpass and you're promising God if he gets you out of this alive, you'll never speed again. I kept my promise, too. I don't speed because, by God, I don't have to. I'm perfectly content to plunk along.

So, Kyle and I begin driving.

I thought it would be a good idea to have a routine that was calming for Kyle, so I began putting a C.D. of James Brown's song "I feel Good" at the beginning of every drive. We would sing along to the music and I was convinced that the repetition of the song helped him focus.

I had read about a famous Autistic woman named Temple Grandin. She listened to music while driving, and it gave me the idea for Kyle. I told Kyle about her while driving. I used her as an example of what he could achieve

"She's a college professor, Kyle. She invented a way for cows to safely go from one place to another by being able to think like a cow. Autistic people have a way of thinking creatively. It's one of their strengths," I said.

"Wow!" Kyle responded.

"If she can do it, you can do it!" I smiled.

So, Kyle would put on his sunglasses and we would take long drives on the country highways listening to James Brown.

We practiced at the parking lot at the High School. I grabbed the door handle and used my imaginary brake on more than one occasion, especially when we hit mountain fog.

"I saw that, Mom," Kyle would say as he watched me out of the corner of his eye.

I would just smile and nervously laugh.

A few months later, Kyle took the test and passed the first time with flying colors.

We were stunned and thrilled! We celebrated with a pizza that night, excited that Kyle had accomplished his first goal.

Even with his driving accomplishment, Kyle was still frustrated at school. He felt the teachers were actually holding him back. Despite his frustrations, he befriended some of the other special needs kids. One kid in particular was a quadriplegic.

Rick and I were driving past the school one day when we saw Kyle. He was racing this boy in his wheel chair and doing wheelies. The teacher was not amused, but I laughed out loud because the boy was laughing and had the biggest smile on his face. We rolled down the window and said, "Hello." They were all walking to Pizza Hut as a special treat during the lunch hour.

Kyle had Gym class with Cat that semester.

The class included mixed grades. She kept him company, and continued to keep bullies away from him. He helped her too. We suspect that Cat is borderline Hypo-Glycemic like I am. She loves sugars and carbs–who doesn't? If she doesn't pair them with proteins, she can get sick or pass out. She knows this, but there were times she would run late and grab a quick piece of toast.

She was running late, and didn't eat breakfast one morning. Gym was first period. The teacher started this day, having the students run the mile as a warm up before weight training. She did it, and she felt alright...until she sat down for the tutorial of the weight room. Her head was spinning, hands shaking, swaying back and forth. Kyle noticed this. She was going to puke, or pass out, and maybe both.

Cat stood up and looked at the teacher. "Excuse me," she said, and ran out the door.

"Hey...where are you going? You can't leave in the middle of class!" the teacher shouted after her.

Kyle got up, and explained to him about her condition, and asked to check on her. He followed and tracked her down to the nearest women's restroom. He then cracked the door an inch. "If there are any ladies in here, I'm coming in to look for my sick sister. So if you're uncomfortable... sorry," he yelled from the hall, and entered the bathroom.

Luckily for him, no one was in this restroom. He found her in one of the stalls, slumped over. She was in bad shape, having thrown up, and fainted on the toilet.

Kyle helped her to her feet, and half carried her down three long hallways to the nurse's office.

The nurse looked up from her computer as they came in, "Oh...set her down here," she said pointing to one of the cots. Kyle set her down, and told the nurse what happened. The nurse handed Cat a small pack of saltines trying to be helpful.

"What's wrong with you? I just told you what's wrong with her! She needs protein, not crackers!" he half yelled at the nurse. He then turned to Cat, "I'll be right back!" and ran out of the office to his locker.

A few moments later, he ran back into the room holding a protein bar, he kept for emergencies.

"Eat this...you know you'll feel better," and handed her the bar. About a half hour later, she felt fine enough to continue the rest of her day at school. They kept an eye on each other for the rest of the semester.

It was during this class that a curious thing happened.

There was a boy in that class that was interested in Cat.

He was short, wore glasses, and was a bit overweight. He would talk to her, get close to her, and even asked her out a few times. She politely rejected him every time. He made the mistake of making fun of Kyle one day, knowing full well that Kyle was her brother. From that day forward, she was polite but cold.

No one made fun of her brother.

One day after gym, Kyle walked up to Cat, after noticing his behavior.

"Hey Cat, why are you talking to that guy?" He asked concerned.

"Well, it's rude if I call him a creeper, and leave. I'm not that mean. Why do you ask? You concerned?" Cat asked.

"Huh, yes. Don't hang out with him, or talk to him too much," Kyle said quietly

Cat stared at Kyle for a minute. "Kyle I wouldn't anyway. There's something off about that guy. Why?"

"Cause he comes around the special needs area, he watches weird anime and cartoons with naked women, and talks about what he wants to do to women. He is nasty, and seriously messed up!" Kyle cautioned.

"Oh, my God! I had no idea. EWW! Ok I'll be polite, but I don't give him the time of day anymore." She stopped talking to him, and eventually he went away.

It was during this time that I was dealing with my own personal demons on prejudice.

I had a relative visit me and we had planned to go to the movies. I wanted to bring both children, but my relative wanted to bring only Cat.

"Why would you want to bring just Cat?" I looked at her confused, as we were driving around the town to see the

WHERE THE ORCHID BLOOMS

tourist sites.

"Well, you know he's a boy and we want to watch girl things. Besides, he doesn't really sees things the way we do," she said.

"What do you mean?" My stomach lurched and I was starting to feel wary.

"You know, he's not like us–not normal. He doesn't feel things the way we do, so he won't even notice," she said light heartedly as she looked out the window.

"Are you OUT OF YOUR MIND? Kyle feels things JUST LIKE US, maybe even more deeply than we do. He just doesn't always let on. He's not verbal. He's very hurt when we don't include him," I said as my voice began to get progressively louder.

"Okay, Okay, chill. We'll invite him," she said, motioning me with her exposed palms to calm me down.

We went to the movies later that day. Afterwards while we were driving home alone, Kyle became really angry.

"MOM, Mom, why do you let her talk to you like that?" Kyle shouted.

Now it was my turn to be surprised.

"What do you mean, Kyle?" I said as I looked at him from the front seat visor.

"MOM! She is SO disrespectful to you, Mom," he fumed. I was shocked.

And then I thought about the day's events. Sometimes in an effort to keep the peace, we let things go. I realized that this relative HAD been disrespectful to me, lobbing one nasty, sly and sarcastic comment after another to me throughout the day, all day long.

I remember thinking, "What is wrong with this picture?

When my AUTISTIC son has to tell ME to stand up for myself and insist on respectful treatment. Wow."

I shook my head and never saw that relative again.

Kyle and Cat returned to school after the Christmas holidays.

Kyle began getting A's and B's in math and science. His math teacher was a constant source of inspiration and kindness to Kyle. Kyle would tell me how she praised his work and would pat him on the back. She encouraged him to help others when he finished with his work. He did and felt a great sense of accomplishment at being the best in something. He looked forward to her class every day. I felt so grateful that there were two teachers in Math and Science who really encouraged Kyle. He became so good at Math, that he started tutoring other students on a regular basis.

"Wow, Mom. I was tutoring some of the other kids today. Some of them are really popular, too," Kyle said in amazement.

"How did that make you feel?" I countered.

He had just come home from school, and I was handing him a choice of healthy treats in a teasing manner: first one then the other as if to say which one DO you want? He absentmindedly grabbed the apple.

"Whenever they said, Thank you, I felt pretty good," Kyle said while nodding his head appreciatively and taking a bite from the apple.

I was so thankful by the progress I saw in Kyle, and all the help he was getting from these wonderful teachers who took an interest in his success.

I watched as Kyle plopped down on the living room couch. He began to channel surf looking very pleased.

He was gaining a new sense of confidence and letting the anger go. He had direction, now and a purpose. He was determined.

I was determined for him.

The plan was definitely working because we had all these wonderful people who were supporting us in our efforts.

No one succeeds in a vacuum. We achieve when people cooperate with us. The trick is to find those people who are willing to work with us and work around the people who won't: the 'naysayers' as I call them.

And, sometimes it's just easier to achieve something first before people decide that you can't do it.

CHAPTER 12

Ranger Amanda and the State Park

The next achievement, or step, was helping Kyle find a job. He applied everywhere in town. No one would hire him. I accompanied him to several places and saw the odd looks that some people gave him as he applied. I was worried because there was nothing I could do other than encourage. Anything more on my part would be emasculating for Kyle, and I was already sensitive to the stares from other people as he applied for these jobs. Still, I sensed that he needed the stability of a calming presence. I justified this by reminding my self that I would have done the same for Cat. I did, later, going with her to apply for jobs and coaching her on the appropriate outfits to wear: nice semi casual slacks in dark colors, white shirt, no jewelry and NO PERFUME.

"No perfume. That goes for you too Kyle. What if your cologne reminds the interviewer of an uncle he hated growing up?" I mocked groaned to their laughter.

I told Kyle that we were new in town. This was a small town and small towns were notoriously hard for "outsiders" to get a job. I told him not to get discouraged. We'd figure something out. Also, he was competing in a tough economy with older workers taking second jobs to feed their families.

When he finally did get a job, he would be very lucky to have one. He needed to appreciate his good fortune.

"Work is a privilege, Kyle," I said one day. "A lot of people see it as drudgery, but life is good when you have work that you look forward to doing every day. Someone really poor would gladly take your place at a job."

Rick and I were working at the State Park during the summers. Rick was the Back Country Ranger and I worked the front gate. Rick's job was patrolling and maintaining the hiking trails in the park. I laughingly referred to myself as the "lowly gate herder", since it was my job to welcome people to the park and direct them to various trails or camping sites.

I often wondered what kind of people worked at places like state parks, and I was amazed at the wealth of experience the workers possessed: retired teachers, avid hikers, artists, retired military and police officers. We often joked with the other workers that no one worked for the money. It was just a privilege to work in such a beautiful place where we could go hiking before or after work.

"Why don't you volunteer at the State Park? If they like your work, they might hire you for a paying job next year," I suggested one day to Kyle.

Amanda, one of the Rangers in charge of the volunteer program, listened to our story. She encouraged Kyle to apply. If Kyle did a good job volunteering, Amanda would write a letter of recommendation for a paying job later.

Kyle became a volunteer and his first assignment was a slide show on Mountain Lions. Amanda praised his work and Kyle beamed under her encouragement. In the meantime, Kyle applied to the Maintenance department but wasn't hired. We encouraged him to continue to volunteer. The busiest weekend of the season, Memorial Day, was about to begin. Rick mentioned this to Amanda and Ron, who was a Maintenance supervisor. Kyle would be willing to work as a volunteer in the field with Maintenance just to help out. Ron agreed.

Kyle showed up expectantly for his first day as a volunteer for Maintenance.

Rick introduced him to Ron and the rest of the Maintenance workers. Rick left Kyle hoping that the day would go well for him.

He rode with Ron on the first day of the weekend to see how the job was done. The man that had originally been hired never showed up. Kyle worked all day and Ron approached me later.

"I worked that boy good," Ron said with a smile. "He never complained once, did everything I said. I told the head of Maintenance that Kyle is the one I want hired."

"Really?" I said. "I appreciate that, Ron. Thank you!" I couldn't believe our good fortune!

He winked and walked away.

Kyle came home excited. "Mom!" Kyle said breathlessly. "Ron told the boss that he wants to hire me!"

"Kyle, that's wonderful. You'd be so lucky to get that job." I said a silent prayer thanking God and Coach for helping Kyle get his driver's license, which was required for a maintenance position. Everyone had to be able to drive a "mule" to haul things around the park.

Rick came home with a grin on his face.

"Ron told me that Kyle picked up his duties quickly and began taking the initiative almost immediately. Ron told me that Kyle was the hardest working guy he had seen in years and that he was going to talk to the head of Maintenance.

The head of Maintenance hesitated to hire Kyle because he was a high school student. He approached Amanda for her opinion.

Amanda came by that day. She said she had gotten a call from Maintenance about Kyle.

"What did you say?" I asked tentatively.

"I told him that if he doesn't hire Kyle, then he's crazy. I know he's been burned in the past from some other high school students who weren't reliable, but Kyle is a super hard worker," She laughed.

I nodded. "Thank you, Amanda. I'm really grateful to you for recommending him."

"Not a problem!" said Amanda with a smile.

Kyle was hired that day.

Rick sat down with Kyle and had a long talk with him.

"This is a golden opportunity for you, Kyle, to show them you're a hard worker. Maybe, just maybe, you could get a good recommendation from the Department Head. So, work hard, don't complain and try to be a team player with the other workers," Rick cautioned.

Kyle seemed deep in thought as he listened to his father.

"Work hard, do 'Good', and make me proud!" Rick started and Kyle chimed in finishing the sentence together. It was the family motto and inside joke.

The head of Maintenance kept a skeptical eye on him through that summer since his attitude was "show me." He prided himself on having the hardest working crew on the park. He told me so one day when he came by the front gate.

"I expect Kyle to work hard for you and to be respectful

at all times. Let me know if you have any concerns. Kyle is very grateful that you've given him this opportunity," I said.

The Boss nodded. He was a bear of a man and kept his own counsel proudly. Some of the gate workers teased him for being a big Teddy Bear. He was kind but had high expectations for his staff.

Kyle blossomed at the State Park. He went from being shy and quiet to joking around with the staff. They teased him constantly in a good natured way.

I would see Kyle driving one of the mules and he would wave to me just beaming. He would come home exhausted but elated. He had a real job.

Amanda would call him over the radio in a very serious manner. Kyle would excitedly hurry to help her only to find her standing with a smile, and a box of donuts, for the maintenance crew.

Kyle proved himself that summer. He also helped Ron quietly when Ron began having difficulty lifting. If Ron over exerted himself, he would temporarily lose his vision. Kyle stepped in and took over the more strenuous duties without ever saying a word to anyone except us.

"Don't tell anyone, Mom," Kyle said to me at dinner one night. "I wouldn't want Ron to feel, you know, embarrassed."

I smiled and marveled at his sensitivity. He was growing up into a kind and thoughtful person.

I asked him, "So what do you think of the people at the park?"

Kyle thought for a moment.

"You know, I think most people are very nice–I do. Most people are friendly," He said quietly.

"Like the campers that baked your mother some cookies,"

Rick said winking at me. "Even after she couldn't get them into one of the cabins."

"I know, but I tried all day to help them. That's why she baked the cookies for me," I laughed.

"The Rangers thought you'd have been strung up a tree, instead of eating cookies. There were a lot of shaking heads in the Patrol room," Rick laughed, helping himself to a biscuit.

"Well," I said, as I encouraged him to a second helping at dinner. "Tell us what you do all day, Kyle?"

Kyle began telling the whole family about his duties and the personalities he worked with at the park. I laughed and told Cat to pay attention since we hoped she would have a job at the park the following year.

"I help clean the bathrooms and showers. We repair campsites. We cut and haul firewood. Sometimes we help clean the cabins or repair them. I like helping to repair the plumbing and the electricity the best. Oh, and the machines. I really like helping to repair the machines. I think the only job I don't like is the painting. I do it, but it's boring."

Rick laughed, "7:30 comes pretty early but at least we get to ride into work together. Hey, why don't you start riding with me at the end of your shift? I'll get permission from the Senior Ranger to pick you up after you clock out from your shift. You can ride the trails with me that last hour. You can see all the trail work I'm doing."

"Ok," Kyle said.

Kyle and Rick hurriedly grabbed coffee and a breakfast burrito the next day, while heading out the door.

This became a daily routine. Rick and Kyle would ride the back country trails and talk about the day. That summer Rick and Kyle became close as they shared stories and compared notes on different challenges on the park. They laughed and compared strategy on how to deal with "unhappy campers" and "grumpy hikers."

"Yeah. I had one grumpy hiker who told me to turn off my mule because the noise was 'interrupting the AMBIENCE of the scenery'. The people I rescued an hour later didn't seem to mind. They were from back east and made the mistake of hiking in flip flop and shorts. When the pellet snow came, as it does in July, they just about froze to death," Rick commented to Kyle one morning as he pointed out the 'lean to' on the trail where he found the hikers shaking and turning blue.

"Oh man! You've got to wear layers in Colorado, and hiking boots with warm socks," Kyle spoke to no one in particular.

Rick guided Kyle on working with some of the more challenging co-workers, as well.

Most of the staff was incredibly supportive and the joking was good natured. There were a few staff members that were not. These people would tease Kyle in a competitive, cruel way. Ron intervened when he saw this, but he wasn't always around.

Rick would counsel him to laugh it off and keep it about the work.

"If they think they can get to you, they'll keep it up. Laugh it off and they'll move on to some other victim, Kyle," Rick encouraged after one particularly hard day. "Consider the source, too. Success is the best revenge, Bud, and someday you're going to be making more money than all of them put together. You watch."

"I get along with most of the workers." Kyle thought for a moment trying to figure it out.

"Listen, you're not going to win everyone over with your hard work. There's no pleasing some people. That's one of the hardest things to learn. Some people just want to put you down to feel better about themselves, and nothing you do will change that. Don't waste your time trying to justify yourself to them or please them. Stick close to the people who support you. Give these people enough rope and they'll eventually hang themselves. You're probably showing them up because you are a hard worker, which only makes them look that much lazier," Rick said grimly

"Well, I get along with the girls," Kyle said with a grin.

"There are some pretty girls working this summer," Rick said with a laugh and looked slyly at Kyle. "Any one girl in particular?"

Kyle laughed.

"Mom says a gentleman never tells," Kyle countered.

"Listen to your mother," Rick growled good-naturedly.

The summer passed sweetly as Rick and Kyle continued to joke, laugh and talk about life while riding the rugged trails of the park. There was a quiet contentment, too, at times when they would ride and just enjoy the setting sun or the shadows on the mountains. They sometimes came across wildlife: elk grazing and baby deer sleeping in the tall brush. Sometimes they caught site of a mountain lion running or a bear swimming in a small pond. They even came across a fox with her kits one afternoon.

Ron came by the gate one morning.

"You've got a good kid, there!" he said absently as he watched Kyle empty some of the trash bins. "He's been a real help to me when I've had problems. Hiring him was the best thing I've done this summer."

I smiled thankfully and nodded as I watched my son with pride.

Kyle felt accepted and part of the team.

At night when he came home, we would sit at the dinner table and discuss the day's events.

Some of the stories were comical. A hiker was seen taking a "dump", as my husband called it, over the side of a rock on an overlook. His naked backside was exposed for the world to see.

"I tried to catch up with him and write him a ticket, but he was long gone by the time I got to the other side of the ravine," Rick chuckled.

"What in the world would you charge him with on the ticket? " I shook my head in surprised disgust.

"Littering," Rick said without missing a beat. "Public exposure, 'Hair 'Ass-ment'."

The kids just started howling.

Kyle shared some stories as well.

"Did you know that the park is supposed to be haunted by the ghost of a guy who was murdered and then thrown down a hidden mine shaft?" Kyle said.

"No, I didn't," Cat and I both chimed in at the same time, our eyes wide with curiosity.

"Some of the campers can be rude, too. We had just finished cleaning one of the bathrooms when some woman came up and said they were disgusting. We had no idea what she meant until we got to the next one we hadn't cleaned. Someone had smeared feces all over the walls. It took us an hour to disinfect it, since it had dried to a hardened crust.

Who would do something like that?" Kyle shook his head while putting down his fork. "It WAS disgusting!"

"That's nothing. I've heard of secret X-rated movies being shot at some of the more remote campsites, secret weddings being performed. One guy left his campsite filled with dolls hanging from a tree and used condoms all over the ground," Rick countered grimly.

"That is truly disturbing. It still doesn't compare with Mr. Fluffy," I said as I chewed slowly on my food.

"Mr. Fluffy?" Cat asked.

"A guy came in one day and said he wanted a campsite for himself and Mr. Fluffy. I smiled and countered, 'Mr. Fluffy?' I was filling out his information on a campsite ticket. He reached into his car and pulled out a stuffed animal which he pushed into my face. I took a step back surprised and shrugged it off. I mumbled something like, 'Oh, that's nice,' when he became disturbed and said, 'No, you don't understand. Inside this stuffed animal are the ashes of my dead cat, Mr. Fluffy. Would you like to pet him?' I coughed and stepped back out of sheer horror as he pushed it closer to my face," I related as I choked down my dinner.

"Have a nice day doesn't cut it, does it?" Rick grinned.

"No. No it didn't," I said widening my eyes.

"You DO seem to get all the weird ones, "Rick teased and laughed.

"I'm at the front gate. It's not like I can avoid them," I countered in mock defensiveness.

"I think the funniest one was from a guy who asked if his daughter could go to the outhouses late at night by herself. Ranger Amanda kept telling this guy it wasn't recommended since she was only five. The camper explained that they were going to camp out in the open so that if a Mountain Lion attacked, they could more easily run to the safety of their car. Ranger Amanda continued to say she didn't recommend that, or that, or that either. I couldn't contain my laughter as she began kicking me to be quiet," I said.

"That's not funny. A mountain Lion has been seen recently. Hell, I saw a bear this morning," Rick growled.

"A bear?" Kyle stopped eating.

"What happened?" I sat stunned. I was terrified of bears.

"Well, I came across one after I parked the mule to check on a trail. I turned around and there he was, just as surprised to see me. You know, he jumped and ran up the hill. He hid behind a tree and then peeked out a few times to see if I was still there."

"You're making THAT up!" I said my mouth dropping to the ground.

"No, I think he was more afraid than I was, and he looked like he was playing hide and seek." Rick was really laughing now with relief.

"Well, I did help one family out. They came very late and realized they couldn't afford to buy a campsite and dinner for their family. The crestfallen look on this man's face broke my heart. So, I mentioned that there were some star gazers looking at the meteor shower that night. Stargazing didn't require a campsite, just a day pass. As long as he stayed awake to watch the stars, no one would notice if his little ones were asleep. The man's gratitude was heartbreaking. He said thank you, as I wrote out a 'one day' pass," I smiled sadly.

"Wow," Kyle whispered.

"Sometimes, I think the rules can be bent just a little to

help someone out," Rick offered while nodding his head at Kyle.

I smiled gratefully.

Sometimes, we would discuss conflict resolution and work strategy with co-workers: the politics and the personalities. We practiced what might work and what wouldn't.

We encouraged Caitlin to apply the following year when she earned her driver's license. It was a wonderful time for us, as a family, to encourage a good work ethic in Kyle and Caitlin. It was also a humbling reminder of how hard most people work just to make "ends meet" or provide for their families. Despite the support that he was shown by his co-workers, Kyle was working on his own personal sense of self worth.

He had just started his senior year of High School. The summer season at the state park didn't end until mid October. He felt plagued by the names that some people called him at school.

Kyle still struggled with an embarrassment over his school Special Needs status. There were times when he was filled with an angry, defensive self loathing. I watched this eat at him day after day.

One day, I surprised him.

"Kyle, do you admire Amanda?" I asked him.

"Yeah, she's beautiful, smart, popular, and she's really accomplished. She's in law enforcement. That's pretty cool," He mused, nodding.

"Kyle, did you know that when she was a child the other kids used to make fun of her because she couldn't read? They would make her cry. She had a reading disability. She can read, but it takes her longer than most people.

She's learned to compensate by working harder, and finding ways to make it work for her. She memorizes many of the things she needs to know," I said.

Kyle was shocked.

He sat there thinking about what I said.

"Amanda just never gave up on her dream to be a Ranger. She believed in herself, and that's why she believes in you," I said solemnly.

"Wow," Kyle whispered. "I had no idea."

"Kyle, someday you're going to be an inspiration to people, just like Amanda will hopefully inspire YOU!" I said. "Amanda figured out a way to make her challenges work for her. She has trouble reading, but she remembers everything she's ever learned almost photographically. We just have to figure out how to make your challenges work for you, because, EVERYONE HAS CHALLENGES!

Kyle's attitude improved from that day forward. Every time he became discouraged, I would remind him of Amanda and the challenges she faced.

"If Amanda can follow her dreams, then I can too," I would hear him say to himself. He continued to thrive as he watched her success and enjoyed her encouragement. He was also the object of good natured teasing because he was "part of the gang" for the first time.

One day, Ron told Kyle to go get a tool at the back of a dark building. Ron then waited for him in the dark and scarred him with a Freddy Krueger mask. Kyle laughed after the screaming stopped. The teasing was a daily gauntlet, but Kyle really felt cared about. These fun and thoughtful people teased everyone who was popular. His sense of community developed to a point where he wanted to reach out and try new things.

Caitlin encouraged him to start coming to the school events with her: the football games and the upcoming dances. She was determined that he was going to enjoy and participate more during his senior year of High School. That summer they took Karate lessons together and dreamed about all the things they would do in the fall. Kyle wanted to learn how to dance if he was lucky enough to have a date for prom. I told him that I would look into lessons.

It was during the end of summer that a tuxedo store was having a going out of business sale. I found a complete tux ensemble for the price of a rental. I took Kyle to the store and had him try on the tuxedo.

"Wow!" Kyle said as he admired himself in the mirror.

"You're going to Prom, Kyle. I just have a feeling. If I'm wrong, you can still wear it to any wedding you're invited to attend. Personally, I think it's good luck to have the tux."

"You think?" Kyle said staring at the mirror.

"Really. You have one of your feelings?" he mused with hope.

"You're going to Prom," I smiled and nodded at his reflection. "Let's enroll you in dance."

CHAPTER 13

Graduation, Awards and College

Kyle and Cat took dancing lessons towards the end of that summer. Kyle wanted to learn to dance for the Senior Prom, and I wanted them to be safe together, so it was a compromise. Kyle often said he wanted to be able to dance the tango like Arnold in the movie "True Lies". I signed both of them up for complimentary introduction dances.

Caitlin complained.

"Mom, why do I have to take dance lessons?" she grumbled.

"Caitlin, it's just three lessons. He needs someone to practice with him. You can do this for your brother!" I barked.

She nodded resentfully.

We all arrived at the studio. Kyle got his first lesson, which was the box step, from the female dance instructor. He grinned awkwardly. I smiled from the corner chair where I sat.

Caitlin was lead onto the dance floor. She began dancing the box step and she was transformed.

I got chills up and down my arms as I watched her walk back, arm in arm, with her instructor after the lesson was over. She was glowing in a way I had never seen her before.

All the way home, she talked about taking more lessons. This was what she wanted to do someday for a living, she loved dance, and it made her feel alive.

"Caitlin, these guys make as much as doctors!" I said. Inwardly, I was horrified. We were still paying off doctor bills. Where would we get the money? My mind raced. I suppose I could sell a kidney, I thought to myself. I carefully approached Rick that night.

"I thought this was just a few lessons for Prom?" Rick snapped as he looked at the sheet of paper outlining the cost schedule for lessons.

"Me, too," I said chewing my lip. "We could still use your salary to pay off the bills and my salary to pay for dance."

Rick nodded throwing his hands up.

I sat the kids down. I didn't think we could afford Karate and Dance. Dance won hands down. Caitlin was just shy of her purple belt, and I would always cry when she challenged for a particular belt. I was so proud.

I soon found I was crying when I watched her dance. She was so graceful that it continually brought tears to my eyes, especially when she danced the Viennese Waltz.

"Okay," I said one day figuring the bills. "We'll all have to do our part. Cat, you'll have to get a job next summer to help pay for dance. In the meantime, I'll pay you for projects to be done around the house. The deck needs painting."

Cat excitedly agreed. Everyday, she patiently painted sections of the outside deck, or cleaned, and I stepped up her allowance.

Kyle and Cat practiced dancing that summer well into fall.

I saw Kyle waltzing one autumn day with one of the older women in Maintenance. They were laughing and twirling. She waved to me.

She came by later to tell me she thought the world of

my son.

I was so grateful for all the kindness she showed to Kyle that year. She became like a second mother to Kyle and watched out for him.

Kyle became more confident everyday. He began going to the communal dances at the studio.

He came home excited one night after a dance party. He had met a beautiful girl.

He described her strawberry blonde hair and said she was the most beautiful girl he had ever seen.

"Hey Cat…Did you know the Pumpkin Spice Lattes are out at Starbucks?" Kyle asked Cat one evening.

Cat looked up excited, they were her favorite lattes. "Huh…no I didn't. I need to get one!"

"Great…let's get one now!" Kyle said

"Kyle it's around 7 o'clock at night, you want one now?" Cat asked quizzically.

"Yes…lets go," he said grabbing his coat.

After going to Starbucks, and getting Pumpkin Spice Lattes, Cat suggested walking around town while enjoying the coffee. It was late October now, and about to snow.

"Thanks, Kyle, for the latte. Now, what's this about?" Cat asked.

"What…" Kyle countered pretending there was no reason for late evening lattes; Cat just looked at him with a "REALLY" look.

"Huh…ok…I really like her, the girl we met at dance. I want to ask her out and take her on a date…but I don't know how to start," Kyle finally admitted.

Kyle and Cat talked for an hour: where and how he should ask her out, what he should wear on their first date, and where to go. Cat helped him strategize, and gave him the confidence to go for it.

Kyle asked the girl out on a date and she accepted.

"Mom, what do I wear? Where should I take her? What should I say?" he rambled distractedly.

"Kyle we talked about this, you know what to do and where to go," Cat encouraged.

He changed his clothes three times, combing and re-combing his hair on the big night.

Cat finally shook her head and went down stairs to give him a "reality check".

The result?

Cat and Kyle walked back upstairs together. He was wearing a nice pair of jeans and a button down shirt with dressy casual shoes.

"Nice job, Cat" I smacked her hand in a high five and nodded my approval.

"This way, you look good, but not like you're trying too hard," Cat said with a final dusting of his shoulders.

"Oh! Oh, splash a little of this old Spice cologne on your neck," I said handing him the bottle. "Girls love cologne!" I smiled excitedly for him.

Kyle laughed nervously and took the young woman out.

Kyle dated her for several months. He went to her church to impress her, and she was very supportive. Her brother was Autistic. Kyle was depressed because she was leaving to go to college. They parted as friends and promised to keep in touch.

Kyle and Cat continued to dance and attend the various dance parties.

Kyle and Caitlin also began hanging around with one of

the other dancers at the studio. She was African American and Cherokee. Her name was Tia. I joked with Cat and Tia later that we could be related through our shared Cherokee ancestry. They became best friends and started going to the dance parties together.

I would sit with Tia's mother at the dance parties. We commiserated on the cost of dance lessons.

"You know, I told my husband that our daughters weren't drinking, drugging or hanging out at the local street corner," I whispered to her one day. "It's worth every penny."

"Mm hmm, you've got that right. That's what I tell my husband too," She laughed, nodding her head.

We were so proud, as we watched our children dance. Week after week, I would stand on the sidelines and watch as Kyle took lessons. He laughed self consciously at his mistakes and laughed when he got the dance moves right. He beamed when some of the pretty dance students talked with him, or danced with him. This was especially true at the dance parties where the girls would often ask him to dance.

Kyle made several attempts to mainstream academically that fall. He spoke to one teacher after another.

The Special Needs teachers called me and advised against it, but relented in the end. Kyle began riding the regular school bus with Caitlin. She watched out for him on the bus. The kids knew he used to ride "the short bus". They would pick on him, bully him, and sometimes physically hit him. Cat would step in and hit back in defense, or tell them to go to hell.

After one gruesome day when the bullying got out of hand, Cat had finally had enough.

She grabbed one guy's lapel, lifting him up, which surprised him because she is so small.

"If you touch my brother again, I will KICK YOUR ASS, and I've got the purple belt in Karate to do it," she said barely above a whisper–just loud enough for the boy to hear it.

Just then three of her friends, who had seen the whole thing, walked up beside her.

"And if SHE doesn't KICK YOUR ASS, WE WILL!" said one of the girls, as the others shook their heads solemnly. One girl helped Kyle up and patted him on the back.

They were ready to "rumble." The adrenaline was high as they eyed each other for a few seconds.

The boy smirked and backed off.

"Yeah, you better go," said one girl.

Another day, in the middle of the school year, the kids were being really cruel, pinching him, and laughing at him, calling him "retard". Kyle just looked at Cat. She walked up and sat next to Kyle.

"Kyle, you need to start fending off these jerks yourself. I'm not going to be here forever. You need to start fighting your own battles."

She stood up and walked to the back of the bus leaving the kids to continue to torture him.

It was a hard lesson, but it was one he had to learn on his own. Cat stopped helping him with the bullies on the bus.

Finally, one day, the kids were doing the usual name calling, pinching, laughing. He hit one guy's hand away, stood up and shouted, "Enough!"

He got right in the face of the main instigator on the bus and said, "If you ever touch me again, I will have you kicked off this bus." He had finally had it. Cat just sat in the back of the bus watching, with pride, as he finally stood up for himself. We all worried less about Kyle from that day.

There was some good on the bus after that incident. Kyle met a pretty girl. Cat encouraged him to ask her to the school dance coming up. Cat also encouraged him to go to more football games and feel part of the crowd. He did and people started saying hello to him. He was becoming more confident.

Rick thought I was crazy when I pulled out the tux we had bought the summer before. I explained to him that I was able to purchase it for the price of a rental, and Kyle would have it for the rest of his life. I smiled at Kyle as I showed him the tuxedo.

"You're going to Prom, I have faith!" I laughed.

Christmas was approaching. Rick and I decided to surprise Kyle by buying him a car, if he got into college.

Kyle applied to Redstone College. It was the College's policy to interview potential students at home to see if the student was a good fit for the program.

A man from the college arrived one afternoon for the interview.

Kyle was understandably nervous.

"Kyle, just be your self," I said, just as nervously as I patted him on the shoulder. And don't tell him you're Autistic. Not everyone is open-minded. Just get accepted, do a great job and THEN tell them you're Autistic. What do you think?

Kyle agreed.

"You're going to do great. I think it's meant to be. After all, you had that dream," I smiled trying to be encouraging.

"Thanks, Mom," Kyle hugged me and smiled unconvinced.

The College interviewer came and sat down at the dining room table. He asked question after question.

Kyle excused himself a half an hour into the interview to get a glass of water. He seemed overwhelmed.

"He's really nervous, isn't he?" asked the interviewer.

My husband and I just looked at each other, and then nodded wide eyed.

"Kyle's not a big talker," Rick said nervously squirming in his seat.

"Dear God. Help us pull this off," I thought to myself as I twirled my thumbs under the table nervously.

"Well, I think Kyle is exactly the kind of student our college is looking to accept!" he said.

"REALLY?" Kyle was shocked.

I was dancing a jig inside. I could barely contain my excitement.

We thanked the interviewer for coming. We looked at each other as we watched him drive off, and then we started screaming. Kyle was jumping up and down; I was hugging Rick and then hugging Kyle.

"OH MY GOD, OH MY GOD, OH MY GOD, I AM SO PROUD OF YOU!" I kept saying over and over.

We began preparing for Christmas a few days later, on Thanksgiving Day. As I mentioned, this is our tradition. Kyle and Rick cook, while Cat and I put up the tree. We had so much to be thankful for that season.

I hung the stockings. Kyle paused to watch me hang his stocking. I had put a tiny matchbox car on the very top of his stocking.

"What's that?" Kyle smirked wide eyed.

"It's a car. Look, Daddy bought you a car," I laughed.

"That's funny, very funny," Kyle shook his head with a smirk.

Several weeks later, we went to town and looked at cars. We really wanted Kyle to be safe so we bought a new car with an extended warranty: a tiny little black Suzuki 4X4.

One of the Rangers took me aside one day.

"Let me get this straight–you're driving an old jalopy and you bought your kid a BRAND NEW CAR?" he questioned me in absolute astonishment.

"Mm hmm," I nodded. "Rick wants Kyle to be safe. It's not just a car–it's safety for Kyle and peace of mind for me. I know I can defend myself if I break down. We don't want Kyle to break down in an old car. We're really buying him 'safety'."

He just shook his head and walked away. He just couldn't understand our reasoning.

Christmas Eve finally came and we hid the car at Grandma's house. I put a huge silver bow on the steering wheel and Rick signed the card which was held by a tiny stuffed pug.

He loved pugs after he saw one sing "Who let the dogs out" in the movie, "Men in Black." The note said, "Merry Christmas, Kyle."

Christmas Eve finally came and Kyle had very few presents under the tree. They were mostly gag gifts: surprise packages with multi-layers of cheese crackers, a soft toilet seat for warmth because of the cold winters in the country.

We laughed as he unwrapped the toilet paper to match.

Caitlin opened present after present.

Kyle seemed 'put out' as he watched her, and decided to go to bed early.

"I'm just busting to tell him," I said to Rick.

"Don't you dare. You'll ruin the surprise," Rick whispered back to me.

"I know, I know, but I feel so guilty tonight. "

"You won't feel guilty tomorrow," Rick tapped me on the knee.

We all piled into the truck the next day with the dogs and headed down to Grandma's house. As we approached the driveway, there was the car.

"Oh, Grandma must have company, Kyle. Do you think you could move that car so we can park the truck? Rick said

"Ok" Kyle replied, still a little blue from the night before.

Rick's mom came out and handed Kyle the keys expectantly as she looked at Rick.

Kyle opened the door, and said in annoyance, "Hey can I move this bow? I can't see to drive.".

Rick shook his head 'no' and pointed to the pug on the dashboard.

Kyle looked at the pug, looked at the bow, looked at the bow again in shock

We all yelled, "SURPRISE!"

"Oh my God, Oh my God" was all Kyle could say over and over again.

Kyle finally got out of the car and hugged Rick. "You guys ROCK!"

Rick laughed and handed Kyle the manual, "Read it. You'll be driving it home tomorrow."

"Oh, Man! Best Christmas ever!" Kyle said surveying his car in total shock.

I hugged Caitlin as it was her turn to look put out, "I promise you, we'll do the same for you as soon as we can."

Kyle and Cat went everywhere in that car from that day forward. They drove the car to school and to parties. Kyle seemed to be on top of the world.

We only had two rules: call us before you come home,
since there is no cell service in several places on the mountain pass, and no drinking of any kind before getting into
that car.

Rick and I enjoy our wine in the evenings, but we explained
that we also wouldn't touch a drop until they were safely home
every night.

"Not one drop of wine is more important to me than you
are. I'll be stone cold sober so that if you get in trouble, I
can come and help you," I said seriously. "But I mean it,
not one drop of alcohol if you have to drive, agreed?"

They agreed. Rick and I felt very strongly that we needed to model responsible drinking in order to get the point
across that this was serious business, and not worth losing
your license over.

"When you turn 21, I'll be YOUR DESIGNATED DRIVER,
and you can go to the restaurant of your choice and try whatever
alcohol you want," I laughed.

"It's a deal!" Kyle laughed.

"Me, too," Cat mockingly begged.

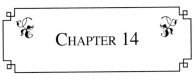

CHAPTER 14

The Tumor Returns

After Christmas break, I got a call from one of Kyle's teachers. She said that Kyle had been going back to the Special Needs classroom and tutoring some of the other kids in math during his breaks. He was doing this quietly on the sly until it came to her attention one day. He was also visiting his friend in the wheel chair who was in the Special Needs program. Kyle and this boy had become friends during their junior year. Kyle felt compassion for him because he was confined to a wheel chair as a quadriplegic. He would visit him at lunch and talk with him. Kyle's teacher was so impressed with his "giving back" to the kids that she submitted his name to the Mayor.

A few weeks later, Kyle had been chosen to receive an award for "Citizen of the Quarter". The Mayor would award him his plaque in front of the town council.

I was shocked. I thanked her for the phone call.

When Kyle got home, I asked him about it.

"I thought you were embarrassed about having been in the Special Needs program, Kyle. You told me that you would never go back once you left."

"I thought about what you said, Mom," Kyle said confidently. "I thought you were right. I need to give back and help people who haven't been as lucky, like Amanda helped me. Whenever you think you have it rough, there's always someone who has it just a little rougher than you do."

I was floored and completely in awe. Kyle seemed so mature and confident now. Silently, I thanked God for all the wonderful people who had helped to transform him. He went from being a resentful, rage filled kid to someone filled with grace and compassion.

Kyle received the award from the Mayor the following week. We watched him as he took the award and shook the Mayor's hand. We all stood to have our picture taken.

"We're proud of you, Dude!" Rick said with a laugh.

Kyle grinned shyly as he looked at the award.

Kyle decided that he wanted to go to Prom a few weeks later. He asked the pretty girl he met the year before while riding the bus.

Kyle came home excited, "Mom, Mom, she said YES!"

"Wow! You're going to Prom." I was ecstatic for him.

On Prom Day, she arrived at our house to say hello and I took pictures. They both wore black with touches of silver and white. They looked stunning and so grown up. Kyle wore a red rose in his button hole and he had given her a corsage.

Kyle said that he had a wonderful time and that it was one of the best nights of his life. He said that, as they danced, it was magical. They ended the evening by raising their champagne glasses filled with sparkling cider to toast the graduating class. He felt like the luckiest guy in the world with a beautiful girl on his arm to share it.

Kyle spent the next few months working hard and keeping his grades up. He was excited about college coming up the following year.

The park invited him back to work the following summer. He was looking forward to making some money and reuniting with all the friends he had made at the State Park.

He continued dating the girl he took to Prom. He adored her, even loved her for a time. Like most high school relationships, though, this one eventually ended. She ended it several months after graduation. Their lives were going in two different directions.

Kyle was hurting.

"Kyle...lets go," Cat said one night.

"Go where? I don't want to go anywhere," Kyle said annoyed.

"Kyle...you need to get out of this house, and I'm the one who's going take you out on the town, just you and me. Now come on, we have to take your car," Cat insisted.

He didn't fight anymore. Cat was stubborn, and if anyone was going to make him feel better, it would be her. They went for a long drive.

Cat began singing at the top of her lungs to a song on the radio. Kyle turned down the music, finding her annoying.

Cat glared at him.

"Kyle...I think you need to just let loose! Yep, that's your problem. You're holding everything inside, and you've got to let it out. It's unhealthy if you don't!" Cat insisted.

"What?" Kyle stated confused.

"Ok Kyle, this is going to sound crazy, but no buts–you've got to do it...ok?" Cat said

"Uh...ok...what?" Kyle said sounding worried. Where was Cat going with this?

Cat looked at him with a big grin on her face. "Ok, I want

you to scream at the top of your lungs, 'BITCH'."

"WHAT?" Kyle said shocked

"Kyle, I'm serious, this will make you feel better. I'll start...BITCH!"

"Jesus, Cat! What the hell!" Kyle scoffed.

"Kyle...Do it." Cat insisted.

"Huh...fine...bitch," Kyle practically whispered.

"Wow...that was pathetic. Who are you talking to...a mouse? C'mon dude, shout it, like you're pissed! SHOUT IT," Cat shouted.

"Bitch," Kyle said loudly.

"Better...BITCH," Cat countered.

"BITCH...BITCH...BIIITCH," Kyle shouted.

"BITCH!" Cat and Kyle shouted together for another minute.

"That really DID make me feel better," Kyle said.

Cat paused for a moment and then said, "Good...now let's get some grub...what do you want?"

The rest of the day they just goofed off. It was healing for Kyle.

The weeks passed and Kyle would watch Cat dance at the Studio. He would wait for her and then drive her home. While they were driving home after practice one afternoon, he realized that he missed dance himself.

"Cat?" Kyle said hesitantly.

"Yeah, dude?" Cat answered looking out the window.

"I miss dance, especially the Tango. You look really good doing it," Kyle said wistfully.

Cat looked over at him. "Thank you Kyle! I appreciate that. Do you miss it?"

"Yeah," Kyle answered.

"Sorry, I wish I could help you." Cat looked at him more closely.

"Could you teach me? Kyle asked excitedly.

"Kyle, I don't know how to teach."

"Well, you know enough to teach me a couple of steps!" Kyle countered.

"Well, I guess I could teach you the basics and a few steps that I know the man's part to..." Cat said mentally thinking of the different steps she knew.

"Thank you, so much, Cat! Kyle said hopefully.

"When do you want to do this?" Cat wondered.

Kyle thought for a moment.

"How about we start this weekend?

"Okay, Saturday?" Cat confirmed.

"Deal," Kyle said smiling.

Kyle and Cat opened the garage door that Saturday morning. They moved some boxes around to the side.

"There, that doesn't look too bad. Now we've got air and a little room to dance," Cat smiled.

They danced together for an hour. Cat taught him the basics and reminded him of steps he already knew. It felt like the first time all over again for Kyle.

Cat finally closed the garage door and moved the boxes back when they were finished.

"So, next Saturday?" Kyle asked with a smile.

"Sure," Cat smiled back.

"Great," Kyle said turning off the garage lights.

Kyle and Cat met at the garage, secretly, every Saturday for a month. It was their private time together.

I sensed that Kyle and Cat needed this time together. They had grown into each other's best friends. I noticed that when anything important happened, Cat always wanted to talk to Kyle first. I saw too that Kyle always weighed Cat's advice with more importance. Cat, more than anyone else, could build up Kyle's courage in a way that made him laugh and feel strong. Encouragement from a parent sounds like nagging sometimes, but from a sister, it always felt like the truth.

Kyle often said that no one told him the truth like Cat. Sometimes the truth is easier to hear when you know that the person telling it loves you.

Rick began taking Kyle out and teaching him how to use a hunting bow. He bought a heavy target filled with straw and taught Kyle to string a bow. I would watch them from the window. Rick would work on sight alignment with Kyle. I could see them laughing and patting each other on the back. Sometimes I was afraid to look when I heard the inevitable, "OH NOOOO!" And then I'd hear laughter again much to my relief.

Sometimes, I would watch Kyle practice archery while his father was working and I would smile.

Rick took all of us to the shooting range. Rick had been a firearms instructor and wanted both children to know how to use a weapon safely, in case of emergencies. He reminded us of a girl whose car had broken down several miles from our house. The girl left her car to get a better cell phone signal and she was attacked by a Mountain Lion. The only thing that saved her life was that her boyfriend pulled up just at that moment and fought it off.

"This isn't the city," Rick growled, "This is a necessary skill in Colorado, and it could save your life when the nearest Ranger is 100 miles away. So, pay attention."

We spent the next few months practicing shooting targets and comparing scores. Rick's Mom even joined us a few times. Rick took me aside and laughed, "We should buy a Zombie target, and I think Kyle will have more fun with this."

I smiled as I watched Kyle practice his sight alignment.

I remembered a story a relative told me when he was a firearms instructor. One of the recruits was failing the firearms qualification. He stood in the middle of the field as, one by one, all the other instructors left. My relative approached him and asked him what he was doing. The man looked at him sadly and said he was praying for a miracle. The instructor smiled and said, "Well, pay attention because God sent ME. Now you have to work on your sight alignment...." The man passed. So many times we are given an opportunity to answer one another's prayers. I looked at my husband with appreciation for all the time he spent with Kyle. We were trying to give him every skill we could to help him before he left home.

Rick reminded him how to pitch a tent and then they did it. He taught Kyle survival skills, and they practiced catching snakes along the lake; how to make an emergency fishing pole out of string and a safety pin, how to find water, how to boil clover for colds, or chew on pine needles for the vitamin C. He showed Kyle the layer of a tree that was edible. I told him about white willow bark and how my Cherokee grandmother said she simmered it to treat headaches; and where there were cat tails, there was always water under the surface. Rick reminded Kyle to be on guard, his head "on a swivel" at all times.

Graduation day finally came.

Kyle had his cap and gown. We headed downtown where

the ceremony was to be held. Kyle seemed tall and proud as he stepped up to receive his diploma. We all celebrated afterward at his grandmother's house. She had bought a cake decorated in his High School colors. I felt things couldn't get any better.

A few days later, the phone rang.

"Kyle, if you'd be willing to start College early, there would be no waiting list. We can get you in early," the college interviewer said over the phone.

"How soon would you want me there?" Kyle countered.

"In two weeks," he said.

"Two weeks??? Okay," Kyle said. He was shocked.

So we scrambled. Rick and I went up to Broomfield and looked at different apartments. We finally found one that had security doors and allowed pets. We were worried about the finances since we had hoped to work that summer to save up for the expenses. Kyle's grandmother saved the day. She presented us with a check that covered his tuition.

"Mom, I don't know what to say," Rick said. He was holding back his emotions and seemed touched as well as embarrassed.

"Just take it. I've been saving and investing for all the grandkids' education for years. I have a college fund for Cat, too. My grandparents helped me and it was the only way I could have gone to college. I never forgot how much I appreciated it, and I wanted to do the same. Someday, Kyle, I want you to do the same for your grandchildren," Ruth said.

"I will, Grandma, thanks sooo much!" Kyle hugged her, visibly touched by her generosity.

We loaded up the car with Kyle's belongings and drove

him to his new home. Rick and I helped him unpack and set his bicycle on the balcony. He looked forward to biking around all the beautiful trails that surrounded his apartment complex. He also intended to bike to the airport near the school, so he could enjoy watching the airplanes take off or land. The bike would prove useful in the event Kyle had car trouble.

Kyle and I did all those things that most of us take for granted the following week. I stood with him while he met with the bank and established an account. He talked with the Electric Company, and the Cable Company to also set up accounts. It was difficult, because Kyle really struggled to understand people on the phone. It was frustrating, but I made him do it, since he would need to know how to do it in the future. He shopped for food and I grilled him on price comparison, just like I did so long ago when he was a young teenager.

Sometimes he would get frustrated. When his stress level reached the boil over point, he would sit in his new bedroom and play video games as a stress reliever.

On one particularly stressful day, I thought he would kill us both during the drive home when he became unfocused.

Now, when I become afraid, I get mad.

"Honestly, Kyle. Driving with you is like driving with a FRICKEN MONKEY," I yelled in exasperation. "Did you eat fish this morning?"

"What?" Kyle said shocked and then hurt. "No."

I was fuming.

"You know you have to eat protein, especially fish to focus, Kyle," I yelled. "And I know this is overwhelming at times, but I'm not going to be here soon. You've got to have a system in place to remind you to do all these things. Part of being an adult is self care!! I won't be here to help remind you to do it."

"Well, what are you going to do, ground me?" Kyle laughed. At that moment, I lost it.

"You know, you have a lot of nerve saying that to me. Your father and I have been very generous with you. Are you paying for this apartment? You're father is working full time to pay for your apartment this summer, and I'll work full time to pay for your apartment this winter. I'm not here for my sake, I'm here for yours. Anytime you're ready to handle this on your own, you let me know," I said quietly. I was seething.

We were both angry by the time we got back to his apartment. The next few days were quiet as we went to our respective "corners" and nursed our wounds. It was stressful.

We eventually apologized to each other. He was learning a new area, and we made several dry runs to his school and to the stores. We found the post office and explored the local mall. I pushed him to know all of these things before he started school. The more comfortable he was with a routine, the better able he would be to handle the stresses of a new school. Routine was the key to his ability to function and excel.

We were decorating his apartment. I was putting all his awards up thinking that it would give him confidence whenever he looked at them. I hung the pictures of Prom and Graduation. I hung pictures of us to make him feel cared about, because I knew I would be leaving soon. I hated the idea of him being alone and three hours away from us.

And then I had an idea.

"Kyle, I want to give you a kitten for your birthday!" I said excitedly.

Our neighbors across the street had a cat. She had just given birth to kittens. Kyle and Caitlin played with them just before he left for school.

Kyle hesitated. He was unsure. Kyle knew that cats can live for 20 years.

"I know you're scared of the commitment, but your cat will be your best friend. She'll watch over you at night. I've even heard of cats waking people up in the middle of the night when an intruder enters the house. What do you say? The cat would be good company and you won't be so lonely," I said trying to reassure him.

Kyle thought about it for a few days and then finally agreed.

Our neighbors had found homes for all but two of their kittens. They had one female left: Cinderella. They gave us Cinderella "free to a good home".

I love my neighbors.

I brought Cinderella up to Broomfield. We took her to the vet. Kyle seemed to have fun playing with her. I made him feed her, to make it part of his routine. We also put on a calendar, right by the front door, a list of future vet visits and all the important numbers that he would need in case of an emergency. I even put the number for the closest pizza parlor that delivered.

Kyle called Caitlin and told her about the new apartment. Caitlin promised to come up and visit as soon as she had a day off. She had begun working at the State Park. She told Kyle how she was able to ride the back trails in the park with her father sometimes, in the Ranger mule. Rick was teaching Caitlin the same things he had been able to teach Kyle:

how to get along with others, conflict resolution, "office politics" and gratitude for a paying job when so many people were out of work and struggling.

"So...Kyle," Caitlin asked. "What are you going to rename the cat?"

"I think its bad luck to rename an animal," Kyle countered.

Cat turned to Kyle. "Kyle...you're a single man with a cat named Cinderella. Are you sure you don't want something more macho?"

Kyle frowned at the realization. "Oh...you're right. I'll just call her Cinders for short."

"Cinders, Cynders. That's a great mechanics name." Cat laughed.

And so it was that Cynders became part of our family. She was a grey and orange tabby with piercing yellow eyes.

She was also a handful. She got into crevices and underneath cabinets. She crawled into the couch and couldn't get out. Kyle had to reach up and find her by listening to her cry. But she was good for Kyle. He had to remember to take care of someone else. He had to feed her and give her water. While caring for her, in an odd twist, he remembered to take care of himself.

I stayed for one month. We continued to make dry runs to Kyle's college, and made lists of all the things he would need to remember. We had his food budget down to 53 dollars a week. We made it a game, and whatever he didn't spend on groceries, he could spend the remainder on fun. We practiced paying bills and how to look up numbers in the phone book: taxi service in case of car trouble, roadside assistance, and a lock smith in case he locked himself out of the car. He was finally getting situated.

He started his first day of college.

"We have a tradition that started with my mother, God Bless her," I said on his first day. "I drive you the first day just like I did when you started Kindergarten. My mom did it for me. I'll be waiting for you at the end of the day with a cup of coffee and a donut. You can tell me all about your first day. Ok?"

Kyle nodded. I could tell he was nervous. He looked at the lunch he had packed that morning and fiddled with it.

"You're going to do great!" I smiled

"I know it's been hard, Mom, but I really appreciate you being here," Kyle smiled back at me.

"I'm so glad that I COULD be here for you, Kyle. I'm sorry for losing my temper at times. Just remember when things get rough, that God loves you. He loves you or He wouldn't have given you to us. We love you more than anything in the world. If you have to go through these things, at least we're here to help. Can you imagine being alone and trying to do some of these things?" I said quietly.

"No, Mom, I can't," Kyle said softly.

"So, GO GET 'EM. I'll be praying for you. Remember, God gave you a viper!" I encouraged him and shook his knee.

He got out of the car and slowly walked to the door of the College.

It was like Kindergarten all over again.

"What if the other kids are mean to him?" I thought.

I burst into tears.

All I could do WAS pray.

"Please, God, help him to do his work. Please give him just one friend, just one person to help and be kind to him. I'm so worried about the unkindness of some people.

Please, Lord, keep him safe."

It's the prayer that every mother on earth says when her child walks out the door.

I picked him up at the end of the day holding the cup of coffee and donut that I had promised him.

"Well? How was it?" I asked with a mixture of hesitation and expectation.

"Wow, it was great! There's so much to learn. The engines are amazing," Kyle said excitedly between bites of donut.

I heard all about his day as we drove home to his apartment. I asked, "So, what do you think of the people?"

"I don't know, it's too soon to tell."

I could see the shadows under his eyes and the sadness.

"You'll make friends, Kyle, you will," I reassured him. "It'll just take time. You'll see," I said.

I was willing it to be true.

The days passed and finally it was time for me to go home. Kyle drove me home through Denver traffic. We brought his kitten, Cynders, with us and Kyle spent the night. Cynders tried to play, unsuccessfully, with our 16 year cat "Baldwin", who wasn't having any of it.

The next day, I hugged him. I told him we were a phone call away. Rick hugged him too. He put in "I feel good" by James Brown, and we waved to him as he drove out of the driveway. I imagined him driving in Denver traffic and started to cry.

I cried for two days.

The first few weeks of college were an adjustment for Kyle. Cynders wanted him to play all night and would scratch at the door. Kyle's days were filled with work. He would call and excitedly explain all the things that he was learning.

"Oh! Cynders has already saved my life. You were right, Mom. She watches over me. I was so tired, that I never heard the fire alarm go off. Cynders woke me up by scratching and throwing herself against my bedroom door," Kyle said excitedly.

"Oh wow, what happened?" I countered.

"Well, let's just say I felt pretty foolish standing outside in the freezing rain, wearing my pajamas and holding a cat carrier in one hand," Kyle yawned from lack of sleep.

"Wow, I'm so glad we got that Cat for you!" I was amazed that she had already protected him so early on. "How is the rest of class going?"

He complained that several instructors got mad at him for asking a lot of questions, while others appreciated his desire to really understand the material. Sometimes he was frustrated about being unable to communicate to one particularly difficult teacher.

We encouraged him to learn as quietly as possible, and to "stay under the radar", as Rick put it, until he had proven himself.

This was not to be the case.

Kyle called one day and said that several guys in his class were picking on him. They were torturing him by showing him pornography in the lunch room and asking him if he was a virgin.

"Wow, what did you say, Kyle?" I asked horrified.

"I told them it was none of their business!" Kyle exclaimed angrily.

"Good. These guys have way too much time on their hands if they have nothing better to do than give you grief, Kyle. Just keep focused on the work, buddy, and stay away from them.

Study and ace those tests. Those guys aren't going to make it through the program if they keep this up," Rick cautioned.

"Have you made any other friends, Kyle?" I asked hopefully.

"Well, I saw one guy walking home and I gave him a ride. He seemed to appreciate it, but a few days later he wanted me to take him to a liquor store.

"What?"

"I just told him that I don't drink. I'm not 21 anyway, and besides I'm not here for that–I have a job to do."

"Good for you, Kyle," Rick and I both chimed in.

"There is one guy, an older guy named "Hank". He's really nice. Sometimes, we sit together and have lunch. The other guys don't bother me when he's around," Kyle said, seeming relieved and grateful.

"He sounds like a great guy, Honey. Stick close to him," I said. I prayed that this man was an answer to my prayers.

"Please, God, just one friend to watch over Kyle," I silently prayed again as I got off the phone.

Kyle came home most weekends. The cat became very adept at traveling, and would make herself right at home in the car. She jealously guarded the downstairs against our cat and the two dogs. She would sit protectively in front of Kyle's bedroom door, swatting at anyone as they walked by. She even swatted at me a few times from under a chair in the laundry room.

I laughed and played with her. When we closed the door to keep her from attacking the older cat in play, she would talk. "Awwww, Come onnnnn, Come onnnnn," she would moan. Eventually I would relent and let her upstairs. I kept an extra close eye on her.

200

At the apartment, the cat loved to play hide and seek. She would hide behind a curtain and peek her head out to get Kyle to play. Sometimes she would peek out from behind a door and swat at your legs as you walked by. Kyle loved her more and more every day. When she began scratching at his door at 5:00 in the morning, however, he would wonder what he had done adopting this cat. I would remind him that she was like any other child and had to be taught manners. I encouraged him to hang in there with her, and that he had to make play time for her so she could run off all that energy.

Kyle began passing his exams at school. He was getting good grades, but still struggled with the paperwork. He would get ahead on the practical parts though, and began tutoring others like Hank. Hank in turn helped him with his paper-work.

Kyle called one day.

"Mom, a teacher asked if I was ADHD."

Uh oh, I thought. "What did you say?"

"Mom. I just told him, no. I have Autism, you know, the low kind so it doesn't slow me down."

I was worried.

"Kyle, I wouldn't tell a lot of people, Honey. Do the work, show them what you can do, and then tell people. Not everyone knows how good you are as a mechanic."

"It's no big deal, Mom. Hey remember that guy I told you about named Hank?"

"Yeah," I responded.

"He said that our mutual friend was asking Hank to take him to the liquor store and buy him alcohol. He wanted to know what I thought. He asked my advice."

"Wow, what did you tell him?" I was surprised.

"I told him that he has no business asking you because he's underage. It's not worth it getting arrested or losing your place at college. I told him that I was sorry, but I decided to distance myself from him at least from this point on."

"Did he agree?" I asked.

"Yep, he's going to distance himself from that guy too. I think that guy is always stoned. I can't afford to hang out with him either."

"I bet it felt good having someone ask your advice, didn't it Kyle?" I laughed.

"Yeah, it DID feel good. He's become a good friend, Mom. He even treats me to lunch sometimes on Fridays. Did you know that he had surgery and couldn't carry his books because he was on crutches? I'm helping him out, Mom. It's no big deal. He'd do the same for me." Kyle seemed awed by this.

"Thank God," I mumbled to myself. "You're a blessing to him, Kyle. Good for you!"

One friend makes all the difference.

The months passed and we decided to bring Thanksgiving to Kyle's apartment that year. Kyle and Rick cooked the turkey. Cat and I decorated his new fiber optic Christmas tree. The tree looked like it was glowing. We decorated it with blue, green and silver balls, which quickly became cat toys. Thankfully, they were plastic and Cynders eventually settled down under the tree, playing with the ribbons.

"Cynders, No!" Kyle would say periodically.

The whole family settled on the couch and floor to eat the feast. There was no dining table since the apartment had only a counter with two stools. He was really lonely when I first left him, but the cat seemed to help immensely.

Having a living thing to come home to at night made all the difference in the world. He was really beginning to enjoy the freedom and independence. "Well, son, enjoy it. Just remember that real independence is earned through hard work. We're working hard to help pay your rent and we're glad to do it, but be careful with the money. How is it holding up?" Rick asked between bites of stuffing.

"It's good, Dad" Kyle reassured him.

We settled down to watch "Miracle on 34th Street", and I made Kyle promise me that he would watch "A Christmas Carol" on Christmas day. Kyle groaned, but agreed.

I sent Kyle care packages and his Christmas gifts. We have a Catholic tradition based on the Advent calendar. He got a "treat" everyday until the 24th of December. I wrapped them all and told him to put them under his tree. He could open one everyday to stretch out the fun.

He opened them all in five minutes.

Christmas came and we celebrated at home.

"Hey, it's been almost 5 years," Rick said one night.

"Oh, wow, we're almost home free," I countered hopefully.

Rick and I toasted the five year mark of Kyle's remission. We felt like we were 'almost there' and very fortunate, as we gazed at the Christmas tree lights and listened to Christmas carols. We were in high spirits that Christmas Eve, as we ate lobster pate and smoked oysters: my maternal grandmother's Nova Scotia Christmas tradition of sea food.

Kyle seemed subdued a few days later while he was packing to return to his apartment.

"What's wrong?" I asked Kyle.

"Mom, my arm...it's back," Kyle whispered.

I was stunned.

My husband and I were terribly wrong.

"This is some 'Christmas', huh?" Kyle said miserably.

I shook my head. We scheduled an appointment in January, and were referred to a specialist who suggested a second surgery.

Kyle took a 6 week leave of absence from school and had the surgery. This was followed by a modified chemo of heavy duty anti-inflammatory medication. The Doctors told us to continue to keep him on only organic meats and milk, to aid the healing process.

The surgeon came out and explained that he kept as much of the muscle as he could, but that Kyle would experience some weakness. Unfortunately, because of this, he had not left a "negative margin". Some of the fibroid tumor was still left behind.

When we saw the Chemotherapist, he rolled his eyes angrily.

"He should have taken all of it. These things always come back." He lowered his voice. "We need to be aggressive. A young boy who just left here had one of these on his chest. It will eventually kill him. Kyle's tumor is traveling up the arm. It could eventually be fatal if left unchecked and reaches his chest.

I swallowed hard and nodded.

We were also referred to another Radiologist. His secretary spent weeks on our behalf, trying to get Kyle's old records from Minnesota. When we got to his office, he proceeded to tell me it had taken him an hour to read Kyle's X- rays, so "I'll have to charge you, but it looks like Kyle can't have anymore radiation."

I looked at him and cocked my eyebrow and looked at the secretary.

"Doctor, I would pay your fee just for your secretary. She has worked tirelessly on our behalf for weeks," I said chewing my lip.

As I walked out of his office, I turned to Kyle and said, "That Doctor is either inept or a liar. It doesn't take ANY-ONE an hour to read an X-ray. But his secretary is worth her weight it gold."

Kyle began heavy doses of anti-inflammatory medicine. He healed enough within a few weeks that he wanted to return to school.

He suffered with continual muscle aches and came home exhausted most days. He was working hard, though, and still getting good grades.

He called one day and said he was thinking about "double blocking." This meant he would be working 16 hour days to catch up.

"Do you think I can do it?" he asked me.

"You're grades are so good, I know you can do it, but you'll have to be very careful, Kyle. You'll have to eat really well and rest as much as you can, or you'll burn out," I replied worried.

Kyle decided to go for it. He worked night and day, finally catching up to his original class. He was glad because his savings were running out.

He made it.

He saw Hank. Hank had spoken to the professor and insisted that Kyle graduate with their class. They agreed and graduation was set for late November.

He told me that he was doing his work one handed more

often than not. He was learning to compensate for his muscle weakness.

He was getting the job done.

CHAPTER 15

*College Graduation, Technician of the Year Award
and Amputation*

Graduation came that November. We were so proud and so grateful. We watched Kyle as he went up to the podium to receive his diploma.

He nervously waved to the audience and said, "Hello everyone."

We laughed, and so did some other members of the audience. It was sweet.

He received "Technician of the Year" award and graduated second in his class.

We were amazed.

We met Hank and his wife. I gave Hank a big hug and presented his wife with a wreath. I had made one for Kyle, as well. It was a wreath of dried flowers decorated with tiny metal airplanes. His wife smiled and thanked me. I thanked them for all the kindness that he had shown Kyle.

"Kyle is a good kid. You know, I wasn't sure that I wanted to be Kyle's friend at first. He seemed a little off, you know," Hank mused.

Hank's eyes filled with tears.

"If I hadn't become friends with Kyle, I would never have graduated. He helped me with the work and helped me when I had hip surgery, to get to class by carrying my books."

Hank glanced around the room remembering. "And HE TOOK A LOT OF SHIT FROM PEOPLE."

I shook my head. We are always given the choice–the opportunity to answer each other's prayers. Sometimes this is presented to us through one single act of compassion or willingness to be a friend. Sometimes, we are asked to overcome our fear to help someone in need, only to find that somehow we were helped in return.

All of Kyle's teachers shook his hand. One by one, they congratulated him and wished him well. Many of them seemed proud of Kyle and a little amazed.

We eventually returned to Kyle's apartment and packed up his belongings. We cleaned his apartment and returned keys. It was bittersweet since he enjoyed the apartment and all his new experiences there. We took one last ride to the college and watched the planes take off at the airport next door.

"I used to come here when I was discouraged and watched the planes take off. It always made me feel better," Kyle said wistfully as he watched the planes.

"You've accomplished so much, Kyle," I said hugging him softly. "And there's a lot more to go. We need to help you study for the FAA certifications coming up: the practical, written and oral exams.

"Yeah, I'm nervous. Some people don't pass those the first time!" Kyle said nervously.

"You'll do it, Kyle. We'll help you study. You'll, DO GOOD, WORK HARD AND MAKE US PROUD," Rick chimed.

Kyle laughed. This was still the family motto.

Kyle took a few days off and we put up the Christmas tree on Thanksgiving. We celebrated Thanksgiving with so much to be thankful for that season. Kyle began studying for the FAA exams shortly after Thanksgiving. We spent those weeks grilling Kyle with study cards. We studied in the car, we studied while cooking. We studied with him in the living room. We all took turns grilling him. Even Cat would test him in the evenings.

Kyle began applying for jobs, pending his certification. He applied to several different aviation companies and daily scanned the internet for job announcements.

We took a break and enjoyed the Christmas holidays. Kyle spent every spare moment with Cat when he wasn't studying, and I encouraged it. They both wanted to take advantage of the time to spend together, before Kyle resumed his studies at the college.

Christmas was quiet that year. We dreamed together and imagined what it would be like when Kyle got a job. Where would he live? Kyle imagined the Great Lakes area or Alaska. I secretly hoped he'd find work closer to home in Colorado. Cat imagined England and possibly moving in as his roommate. She wanted to travel with Kyle. The dreams seemed to take on a life of their own as we talked around the lights of the Christmas tree. Anything was possible.

New Years came and we hugged each other for good luck, hoping to be together the following year. I sang Auld Lang Sine and cried, just as my grandmother had done when I was a child. I never understood the bittersweet words of the song until she passed away, and I sang it in memory of her, just as she sang it for her mother and father.

New Years day brings with it so many memories and so many wishes for the future. Our family was no exception. We prepared to travel to the college for the second phase of

Kyle's exams.

We drove back up to the college for the dreaded Written Exams.

Kyle passed on his first try! We were ecstatic: one down and two to go.

Kyle's other exams were scheduled for late January and February.

It was a few days later that Kyle got a phone call.

"Kyle, it's for you. It's Lockheed Martin," Rick said as he handed the phone over to Kyle.

Rick's eyes were huge with anticipation.

Lockheed Martin was located in Georgia and the company was looking to hire several Air-Frames and Power plant mechanics. They called Kyle and scheduled a "telephonic" interview with him in the following days.

Rick and I spent the next few days quizzing Kyle with possible interview questions. Preparing for an interview is helpful to anyone, and for Kyle, it was crucial. The repetition and practice was very calming for him when dealing with his Autism.

When the call finally came, Kyle took it downstairs for privacy. Rick and I held our breath upstairs waiting for the news. We knew Kyle was nervous.

Who wouldn't be nervous?

WE WERE NERVOUS.

Kyle eventually came upstairs.

"Well???" we both chimed at the same time.

"It went well," Kyle said, nodding his head up and down, pleased with himself. "They said they would contact me to reschedule a second face to face interview at their facility in Georgia. They'll pay for lodging and the plane ticket."

We were stunned.

Georgia. It had never come up in our Christmas fireside dreaming.

Rick decided to accompany Kyle, since he had never done any traveling on his own. Even though Rick would be with him, he made Kyle do everything so that he'd be prepared to do this again. Rick also thought that he could help him prepare for the second interview.

The time came, and Rick had Kyle check in at the airline. Kyle found the departure gate and found the way to the car rental facility at the airport. He rented the car and they drove to the motel. Kyle felt very confident as he checked himself and his father into the room.

Rick called me later that evening.

"Hey, you'd be really proud of your son. He did everything, and it all went without a hitch. We're going to take a dry run to locate where the interview is going to take place tomorrow morning. I don't want to chance rush hour until we have an idea how far this is from the motel. I'll have Kyle drive it tonight, but I may drive it tomorrow so he can concentrate on the interview."

"That sounds like a good idea," I replied. "This will give him a chance to familiarize himself with the route, but he won't get over stimulated tomorrow by driving it."

"Exactly!" Rick agreed.

Kyle drove to the company, and as they were driving back, Kyle saw a brand new F-22 Raptor take off, right over the car, with an F-16 Chase plane. It was an awe inspiring end to the day.

They spent the rest of the night eating take out and preparing for the following day's interview.

The next morning, Kyle dressed in a suit and tie. Rick helped him adjust the tie and smiled at him.

"I'm ready," Kyle said to his father. He had a can of tuna for breakfast to help his concentration.

They drove to the interview. Rick waited with Kyle and noticed some of the other applicants waiting in line outside. Rick was shocked.

Only two other people were dressed in a coat and tie. The rest of the people were dressed in casual street clothes. One person in particular, was dressed in a tee shirt and blue jeans!

Kyle was the best dressed man there. Rick marveled at the casualness. This was an interview for a possible career, and first impressions meant everything.

Rick returned to the motel room and waited for Kyle's call.

Kyle called three hours later. Rick picked him up.

"How'd it go?" Rick said as he opened the door for Kyle.

"Pretty well. I think it went pretty well," Kyle said hopefully. "They said they'd call me back in a few weeks after a mandatory background check is done."

Kyle seemed elated.

"I'm really proud of you, Kyle. You were the best dressed man there," Rick mused.

They returned to the motel. Kyle checked out and then drove back to the Atlanta airport. Kyle turned in the rental car and then boarded the plane. They flew home.

Kyle was tired but happy when he arrived home.

I had made a special dinner that night to celebrate. It was Kyle's favorite: Split Pea and Ham soup.

"Hey!" Kyle kissed me as he came through the door. "What's this? Mm!"

Rick scowled. He hated Split Pea.

I laughed as I mouthed to him silently in mock anger, "It's for Kyle."

We gathered around the fireplace and I gave each of them a beer.

"This is a celebration," I gushed. "What did you think of Georgia?"

"I liked it. I did see some really poor places, though." He took a sip of beer thoughtfully.

"Well, Southern girls are very pretty and polite. My paternal grandmother was from the south–Tennessee. Manners mean everything in the south," I encouraged.

Kyle smiled indulging me.

"I admit it! I want grandchildren," I laughed.

"Well, don't be in too much of a hurry. Kyle's not married yet," Rick groaned.

"I think you'd like it there, Kyle. The people are friendly for the most part, and the weather is beautiful. The days are warm and muggy most of the year." I tried to encourage him and myself. Georgia seemed so far away.

"We could do some great deep sea fishing," Rick smiled at the thought.

"Well, I don't have the job yet," Kyle said, chewing the side of his cheek.

"I'm going to pray that you get the best job meant for you, Honey, with nice people to work with at the plant," I said quietly.

The weeks passed and we waited.

I was in the kitchen when Kyle came to me a few days later.

"Mom, the tumor is back. I'm in a lot of pain," Kyle said, as the tears streamed down his face.

I felt cold inside, as I nodded sadly. I tried not to let the

WHERE THE ORCHID BLOOMS

horror of what was happening show on my face, as I gave him some anti-inflammatory medicine.

We scheduled another Doctor's visit. The oncologist shook his head. He referred us to another specialist up in Denver, as a last ditch effort to save the arm. His only option was experimental treatments. We tried several of these over the next few months. It was Kyle's last hope.

The oncologist was supportive, but cautious, and referred us to a surgeon.

Dr. Wilkins, I was told, was one of the best surgeons in the country. He was a gentle mannered, good natured man who made Kyle laugh.

I became desperate during this time. I even arranged for Kyle to see a hypnotist. Kyle lasted two sessions and then became frustrated, because she had her own agenda of finding Kyle's "root psychological pain" in order to release it, rather than guiding him to direct his body to heal. By this time, Kyle was in so much pain, he couldn't relax and go into a deep trance anyway.

I was so angry that there were nights I raged against God. "ENOUGH! ENOUGH ALREADY!!! HE HAS AUTISM. NOW HE'S GOING TO LOSE HIS ARM? HASN'T HE SUFFERED ENOUGH? NO MORE, NO MORE. PLEASE!"

I alternated between begging and fury. I cried watching his pain. Most nights he couldn't sleep, and he required more and more drugs to function.

We realized the experimental drugs weren't working after a month. We went back to the surgeon feeling absolutely defeated.

"Well, he can't use his arm and he's in pain," Dr. Wilkins said. "It seems that the only option left is amputation."

The tears began streaming down my face. I just sat there looking at the wall. Dr. Wilkins kindly handed me a tissue. We had all worked so hard to help Kyle save his arm, and Kyle had suffered so much. I wondered if it had been worth it, putting Kyle through all of the drugs, without knowing what effect that they would have on his future health. Was it all for nothing? Maybe we should have let them take his arm years ago. Why did we fight so hard? Was it worth it? All these thoughts raced through my mind, as I sat in that Doctor's office. Still, I knew that Kyle's quality of life was miserable. It was time to face the hard, cold truth. There was no alternative: amputation.

We drove home in silence. When we got home, there was a message on the answering machine. It was Lockheed Martin in Georgia.

They offered Kyle a job in their Georgia facility.

We stood there around the phone in stunned silence.

Kyle called them back and quietly explained that he was having surgery, so he would not be able to accept the position.

"Oh, what kind of surgery?" the girl over the phone replied cheerfully. "Maybe we can reschedule your starting date?"

"I'm having my arm amputated," he said quietly.

There was silence for a long time and then the girl said, "Oh. Okay—well call us back in the future when you've recovered."

"Thank you," Kyle said quietly as he hung up the phone.

I had never seen Kyle look so low.

It was the end of May. The surgery was scheduled for early morning the following week.

The day we dreaded finally came. Kyle's eyes grew wide when he saw the needle they were going to use. The nurses and doctors were upbeat and encouraging. We stayed with Kyle as long as we could, then hugged him goodbye and wished him well. We went down to the waiting room, and then decided to get something to eat at the hospital cafeteria. We sat in silence, eating, when Dr. Wilkins appeared. He seemed surprised we were in the cafeteria. I felt oddly guilty, as I looked at my plate and then back up to the doctor.

I smiled weakly, mumbling something about low blood sugar and passing out if I didn't get some protein. I felt the joke fall flat, even though he smiled.

He said that he wanted to use stem cells to rejuvenate the arm's healing process. He needed our permission to use them, and explained that the stem cells came from donated umbilical cords.

"I see no ethical dilemma, Doctor, and, if it will aid the healing process, then I'm all for it," I said, as I played with my food. We signed the papers.

We finished eating and headed up to the waiting room. Rick read and paced. Caitlin and I played cards and read. Sometimes we looked away and cried, all in our own turn.

A man came into the waiting area and began talking loudly on the phone during this time. I had the sense it was a show for our benefit. The man hung up the phone loudly and asked us for money, claiming to be short for the cab fare home. He said he was a cancer patient, but he had a defiant and aggressive attitude as if he was entitled to the money.

I looked at Rick miserably. Rick became angry.

"We can't help you," he muttered forcefully.

I looked away, feeling as if he had intruded on our grief to pan handle. I didn't believe him and felt disgusted.

We waited and we waited. We looked at the clock as the

hours passed.

"What if Kyle doesn't make it?" I asked to no one in particular.

"We just have to hang in there, and have faith," Rick mumbled.

"FUCK GOD. I WANT MY SON. I WANT MY SON. I WANT MY SON TO LIVE!" I felt an overwhelming rage start to build in me. I was shaking with it.

I had completely lost my faith on an emotional level. I only knew that I wanted Kyle to be healthy, happy, and WELL! I wanted him to have joy and a family someday. I wanted him to live, and I didn't care about God's end game. I didn't care about some divine plan. I was just tired of seeing him try and try, only to suffer over and over again.

I started to cry.

Rick leaned over and held me.

"Are you sad because you regret what you said?" Rick whispered.

"No. I'm sad because I meant it," I sobbed.

The doctor came out several hours later.

We had been fearful. I couldn't imagine losing my son. Images of him flashed before my eyes–of his first steps, his laugh, his experiments and fishing expeditions. I was really afraid of the severity of the surgery.

"Kyle did fine. The amputation surgery was successful, and you can go see him in a little while. Kyle said I can use his arm for research. He said if I could help someone else, then, 'ABSOLUTELY, be my guest,'" Dr. Wilkins smiled, appreciating the gesture.

We thanked him for all his hard work and efforts on Kyle's behalf. He seemed surprised. We knew he had done everything he could do to save the arm, and we were grateful, despite the outcome.

When we could finally see him after the surgery, Kyle was heavily medicated, but awake. Caitlin walked over to his bed. Kyle looked at all of us and said, "Hi, I'm Mr. Stubby!" waiving his bandaged stub.

Caitlin laughed and, from then on, called him Stubby.

Rick stayed with him the first night, while Cat and I spent the night at my mother-in-law's.

We came back the next day, and I spent the next night watching over Kyle. He was heavily sedated and needed help. I was glad to do it. He was very unsteady and almost fell several times. I couldn't imagine him being alone.

Kyle thanked me, over and over, for being there for him.

I kissed his forehead the way I had done when he was a baby. I had to fight back the tears.

"I'm glad to do it, Kyle. As long as I live, I'll always be here for you," I said.

Inside, I alternated between gratitude that Kyle was alive, and resentment that this hard working kid, who had overcome so much, was still suffering. I fought against the bitterness creeping into my thoughts.

Rick raged and I nodded.

"Rick, if we lose it–if we don't hold tough, then who will be there for Kyle? I agree with you, but we've got to keep it together for Kyle. We've got to encourage him. It's not his job to take care of US emotionally," I cautioned.

Rick was grim, "I know you're right, but something has to give. The kid's been through enough."

All I could say was, "I know, I know. On an emotional level, I agree with you. But I've had time to calm down from the other day. TODAY I CHOOSE to believe that there is a higher purpose to this experience, for Kyle's sake–a higher purpose for Kyle and other people. I CHOOSE to believe that God will use this to, somehow, make life better, easier for other people. I just don't know how yet. Do I really FEEL this way? No, I don't, but I CHOOSE to believe it anyway. There has to be meaning, some good to come out of all this suffering–otherwise, what was the point? God can't be that cruel. I have to believe that, for my own soul's sake."

We sat there in silence for a few minutes.

"I choose..." I mumbled under my breath, "to believe, because if I don't, I won't be able to make it through one more day."

We finally took Kyle home.

He slept for most of that week. Eventually, he came out more and more. He struggled to do most things that people take for granted with two hands: tying his shoe laces, buttoning a shirt, cutting chicken. It was new territory for all of us.

I looked at Kyle's shoes and decided that the first thing I would do was to get slip on hiking shoes that could be laced with one hand. They were skid resistant, and Kyle wouldn't have to fuss with constant readjustments. Kyle did learn to tie his shoes with one hand, and I marveled at his ingenuity. He learned to compensate so quickly. Some things eluded him and seemed impractical: de-veining shrimp or de-boning chicken. I bought him clip on ties. These things seemed impractical when it was so easy to get these things pre-done. He did work for weeks to relearn how to play video games, and finally came up with a brilliant idea.

"Gross!" Caitlin said as she crinkled her nose.

"Hey it works. Want to play?" Kyle countered, offering her his Xbox controller.

Kyle was playing with his lips and his tongue.

I had to laugh as I saw them sharing the controls. Cat would wipe them down with baby wipes when she took the controller from Kyle. Now it was Kyle's turn to be grossed out, since he didn't like the taste of baby wipes.

Everything is compromise, isn't it?

We went back to Dr. Wilkins.

"Are you feeling depressed?" asked Dr. Wilkins.

Kyle looked surprised. Dr. Wilkins mentioned that some people felt that losing an arm was like losing a best friend.

"Best friend? It was like saying goodbye to a bully. I can finally get a good night's sleep now," Kyle laughed.

We began a series of occupational and rehabilitation therapies. Sometimes it was twice a week in Denver, which was 2½ hours away, one way. Some days we just seemed to live in the car. We calculated doctor's appointments to avoid downtown Denver rush hour traffic. We succeeded most of the time.

Kyle and I used this time to talk and dream. I began buying CD's that we could listen to on those long car rides: Ozzy Osbourne, Aerosmith and Jethro Tull–"Heart" and "Gun's n' Roses".

"Mom, you like METAL?" Kyle was amazed.

"I don't like the misogynist kind, but some of it I really like. Let that be our little secret," I winked back as we weaved in and out of traffic.

Denver traffic, like most big cities, is not for the faint of heart. The music bolstered our courage and our resolve to overcome the traffic as well as the rehab.

"How do you think it's going to be?" Kyle asked me one day.

"It's going to be a lot of hard work! It's going to suck eggs some days, but it's got to be done. What's the alternative? On a positive note, you're really good at mechanical things. I'll call you my Terminator man," I answered with determination and a smile, while opening my eyes wide to make him laugh.

Rehab was slowly coming to a close. Kyle got his first temporary arm. He spent the next few weeks trying certain things. He fooled with the tension on the rubber bands. He practiced grasping and holding to various degrees. He dealt with muscle ache and fatigue, which sometimes caused accidents.

Spills were usually lapped up by our grateful collie, and she began following Kyle around, hopeful, much to his annoyance. Our German Shepard, Aslan, followed the collie. It was comical to all but Kyle.

"Mom, I can't believe how primitive these things are made. Look at this!" Kyle was exasperated, holding out his temporary prosthetic one day. "It's just made out of nuts and bolts, tiny pulley systems, and plastic," Kyle said.

"Kyle, on pain of death, you are not allowed to take that arm apart. I mean it, Honey. We can't afford it. Maybe in a few years, you can take an old one and see how it works. Promise me–because any tinkering will null and void the warranty on that arm," I said forcefully.

"Okay, Okay," Kyle laughed as he made the sign of the cross with one finger and his prosthetic as if to ward off a vampire.

"Someday, maybe you can design something better, Kyle. It would be wonderful if you could design something more affordable. I don't know how young parents of small children afford these prosthetic limbs. We're looking at $3,000.00, WITH insurance, and the arm has to be replaced every 3-5 years. What do people do without insurance, since the bottom of the line is $10,000.00 without health insurance?"

"You know, maybe with my education on fabrics and metals from working on airplanes, I could design and build something better," he said.

"God, I hope so," I nodded.

I started calling Kyle "Skywalker" after Cat teased him one day. She blew in and out of her hand, "KYLE, I AM YOUR FADDER."

It was so out of the blue, that we all just howled. We were in the kitchen making dinner.

"No, no, I prefer Stubby," Kyle said.

"So, what are you going to tell people about how you lost your arm?" I asked giving him a bite of salad.

"I don't know." Kyle thought about it.

"You can tell them that you should never wrestle a bear," Rick laughed.

"Oh, or, that sharks don't like being petted," Cat added.

"Never play with a mountain lion," I chimed in.

"I'll just tell them that I got tired of it one day and decided to trade it in on a new model," Kyle laughed.

"I think you should change your story every time and make it a running joke," I mused.

"Yeah, like the fish story that gets more and more 'wild' as time goes by," Rick said.

"Kyle, if you're not uncomfortable, and if you laugh, everyone else will relax too," I said between bites of dinner. "People are naturally curious and they will stare. Just put them at ease. You set the tone. If it's no big deal for you, then it won't be for others."

"What do you think girls will think of this?" Kyle said quietly.

We all stopped talking.

"Kyle," I said after a few seconds. "Any nice girl will see you, not your arm. You wouldn't want to be with anyone so shallow that they couldn't see past it anyway. There's someone out there who is perfect for you. You'll find her someday, I promise–someone like Tia, or how about one of those nice girls across the street?

I chewed my lip thoughtfully.

"Of course, they're Church of the Latter Day Saints and I'm a wine drinking Catholic. I may never see my grandchildren," I teased.

"And, if not, there's always ME to keep you company!" Cat shouted while smiling wide pushing out her teeth. Kyle groaned in mock pain at the thought, but smiled later.

We continued with therapy to use the temporary arm. Sometimes we would stop for bagels at the hospital for lunch. The months passed.

Kyle and I had some of the best conversations about life and dreams during those car rides. It became our special time to imagine new inventions and science fiction, and singing along to music. I cherished every day.

Finally, the day came for Kyle to get his new, permanent arm. It was during the Christmas season.

He tried it on and a man from the prosthetic company helped him to adjust it.

"Merry Christmas!" I laughed. "Maybe we should decorate it with garland or put fancy racing stripes on it."

Kyle admired his new arm and tried it out for good measure.

"Not bad," he mused as he adjusted his arm and moved his chest muscles.

We left and got into the elevator. An elderly couple tried hard not to stare. They were unsuccessful.

Kyle moved his arm, "It's my Christmas present. Pretty cool, huh?"

The couple started to laugh and nodded.

As we got to the car, I said, "That was perfect. The way you handled that situation a few minutes ago. I'm proud of you."

Kyle hugged me. "Thank you so much for helping me with all this."

I nodded and hugged him back.

"I think you should start driving again. Your permanent license is coming up in a few months. You need the practice before the test at DMV. They may make you take a driving test with your new arm. I hope not, but you just never know," I said thoughtfully, chewing my inner cheek.

Kyle began practice driving and did really well.

"I've been driving mostly one handed for the past year anyway, Mom," Kyle shrugged.

Dr. Wilkins took a look and nodded one afternoon.

"He has a fine range of motion. There's no reason why he can't drive. You've really mastered the arm in a short amount of time. Just make sure it's an automatic transmission," Dr. Wilkins said. He seemed surprised and impressed.

Kyle practiced a few more weeks.

His 21st birthday came and Rick took him to the DMV.

The guy at the DMV took one look at Kyle, scratched his

head," You'll need a note from your doctor verifying that you can drive–NEXT."

I scheduled an appointment with his General Practitioner. He examined Kyle's arm, watched him move it. He weighed Kyle. Kyle came back to the waiting room while the doctor walked away deep in thought.

I peeked around the corner and saw him looking up at the ceiling, smiling.

He emerged a moment later with the DMV paperwork.

"I think it would be best if you had the DMV give Kyle a driving test to determine how well he can drive, for liability purposes. You'll be glad you did it this way," He said grinning with nervous condescension.

Kyle and I stared at him blankly.

I took the forms silently and nodded grimly.

We got outside and Kyle erupted, "What a Jack Ass!"

"Kyle, we'll never go to this doctor again. He never asked you to show him if you could drive, he just gaffed us off after 5 minutes. If he had been unwilling to sign these forms, he could have told us that over the phone. He wasted our time for $35.00. Don't worry, we'll work this out!" I was seething.

I got home and I was furious. I began to workout on the treadmill to let off the steam that was building with every moment that I thought about his words. I was so angry that I just kept working out while talking to myself–Pencil Pushing Geek, Son of a Bitch, High school Nerd with a Napoleonic Complex, Jack Ass, and I'LL THANK HIM? LIABILITY? HIS LIABILITY, YOU MEAN, Spineless Wimp, Bastard!

Rick came home. He walked down the stairs to see me

furiously working out, "What is going ON?"

"I'll tell you. That nervous little dweeb refused to sign off on Kyle for the driving test. He could have told us he was unwilling over the phone, but instead he weighed Kyle. He looked at his arm for 5 minutes, just to get his fee. A fee I would gladly have paid, had he just truly tested Kyle. Can you believe this?" I grumbled loudly.

Rick shook his head disgusted, "Call Dr. Wilkins."

I nodded continuing to burn off my rage on the treadmill.

"We have come way too far to allow this little jerk to stop us!" I yelled.

Rick called Dr. Wilkins and his assistant answered.

"Sure, we can do that. We do those all the time. I have his chart right here. He just has to use an automatic," she said cheerfully.

Rick and I decided to proceed quietly to make sure that the General Practitioner wouldn't interfere. We drove up to Denver and got the paperwork from Dr. Wilkins office.

Rick took Kyle back to the DMV. They took a look at his past driving record (no accidents) and the Doctor's note.

Kyle got his permanent adult driver's license without a hitch. He beamed as he walked out the door and showed me his picture.

We signed up for a new General Practitioner the next day, for the whole family.

"Rick, I want someone who will make the tough choices for me when I'm on a hospital gurney someday–choices that are best for MY well being and not for his legal protection. He can cover his ASS on someone else's dollar. I'm done!" I fumed.

Rick said, "I hear you–it's done."

And just like that, we had a new primary doctor.

Kyle enjoyed his new found freedom. He began driving again, and we started working on the up coming oral exams for the FAA. We grilled Kyle at all hours of the day, even while driving in the car to get him used to potential distractions.

"You've got to know this, Bud," Rick said forcefully, one day while driving." You've got to know this like the back of your hand to pass."

Kyle called the college and arranged to go up and practice for the Practical exams. This was the final part of the Certification test.

Week after week, he practiced his skills. Redstone College was more than helpful, allowing Kyle access to the machines. We were so grateful and impressed with the head of the faculty. He was so supportive that he even gave us his personal number, in case we had any problems.

One day, while Kyle was practicing with his prosthetic, his instructor introduced him to two men from the FAA (Federal Aviation Authority). Kyle looked up self consciously.

"I'm sure you have a lot of guys like me in the industry," he said smiling self consciously.

One of the FAA inspectors opened his eyes wide and responded, "Actually, Kyle, we don't."

Kyle related the story to us later that night. "I think they were impressed, Mom."

Kyle continued to work with the makers of the prosthetic, and had a special attachment built called a "bucking bar", which allowed him to do his work well and effortlessly. The prosthetic had to be able to lift at least 75 pounds in order for Kyle to work effectively as a mechanic.

"I want the work to look GOOD, Mom," Kyle said with

pride.

I understood. In his own way, Kyle was an artist. He took pride in making the rivets beautifully installed, or the fabrics smooth. A flush fitting rivet is important in the building of an aircraft, because it reduces drag and, therefore, increases speed and reduces fuel consumption. This increases an airplane's range. He also would point out smooth filings and sanding that made the body beautiful to the eye. He would smile at a paint job, and take pride in the fact that the paint was smooth and without air pockets or runs.

He worked tirelessly for several months and prepared for his final exams.

The day finally came. We drove up to the college listening to 'Crazy Train'.

"I like this," Kyle said nodding his head to the music.

"Yeah, it's Ozzy Osbourne! It's powerful and it'll give you confidence, Kyle," I laughed. The next song is by Jethro Tull.

Kyle laughed too, but I could tell he was nervous.

"You'll do great! Remember, it's a game. No matter what, you'll do it. I don't care how many times you have to take the tests. You'll do great on the Practicals–you've always aced those. The Orals, just breathe deeply and ask them to repeat the question, if necessary. You can do it, Baby. This is the LAST hurdle," I said cheering him on.

I was hoping this was true, and that he would pass on his first try.

I dropped Kyle off and went shopping. I passed the next six hours window shopping, until I came across a machine that made dog tags. I smiled as I had them inscribed with the words "Skywalker, A&P Mechanic", and the date. I took a step in faith that he would pass. I also picked up Guns and Roses "Welcome to the Jungle." I hoped that it would give me strength. We would be driving home in rush hour traffic, Denver style–you know: no signals, weaving in and out, other drivers driving like walking with 2 inches off your back bumper, while texting on the phone.

You know, MAYHEM.

Kyle came out of the college later that afternoon looking blank.

Oh no....

He got into the car and stared out of the window. Then he smiled and cocked his eyebrows.

"I PASSED, first time, oh yeah." He swayed back and forth.

I started to scream, "YES, YES, YES, YES, OH MY GOD." I grabbed him and started hugging him again and again.

We laughed. I gave him the gifts. He put on his dog tags and asked if he could drive home.

"Sure," I said." And here's a little something for your listening pleasure."

"Oh! What a great song!" Kyle said surprised.

"I know. It's the best song ever for rush hour traffic. It's called 'Welcome to the Jungle' by Guns and Roses," I said, nodding to the music.

We rocked to the music all the way home. We felt happy. We felt hopeful. We felt so grateful.

I thought of all the people who had helped Kyle. I reminded myself that no one succeeds alone. We all have cooperation and help along the way from others. I wondered at all the people that had come into Kyle's life, at every point that he needed help, like angels sent from God.

I remembered all the people who were like stumbling blocks, refusing to support our efforts, because they were either fearful or had their own agendas. Some were just grimly prejudicial–seeming to resent Kyle for all his successes, taking an odd pride in the power of questioning his ability to do anything "normal."

Normal. There's no such thing. There's only the common place and the uncommon. Everything seems to deviate on some level, making all of us unique. Isn't that the point?

We celebrated that night. We planned strategy for the future, over pizza. We dreamed and we laughed. It was one of those perfect days.

It didn't last.

The days passed into weeks. The weeks passed into months. Kyle would sit next to his computer and apply for jobs. The tediousness was grinding, and Kyle would end the days exhausted.

Kyle would play video games and hide in his room on the weekends. It was a way to relieve the stress.

I became frustrated, because I knew that being cooped up in the house wasn't healthy. Kyle needed to get out and use his education in order to keep his skills current. We began looking for places that Kyle might be able to volunteer as an airplane mechanic. We toured several small airports, but Kyle felt like an oddity. He felt the other mechanics weren't all that welcoming.

Kyle's birthday was approaching. Kyle's grandmother had an idea. She called one day and offered to give Kyle flying lessons for his birthday.

"Mom, that's a great idea," Rick said over the phone. "It's just what Kyle needs."

We took Kyle for his first introductory flight at an air-field near the Air Force Academy. We toured the facility as, Kyle's eyes brightened. We watched him take off with an instructor, and we watched as he flew back and forth across the field.

"Mom, this was such a great idea. Thank you, so much. I can tell this really lifted Kyle's spirit," I said.

"Glad to do it, Donna," Mom said. "This guy has worked hard and he deserves a break."

I smiled. Ruth was incredibly supportive in a no-nonsense, "get the job done", way. It sometimes reminded me of the 1940's attitude that was a matter of fact practicality and admiration for hard work. I admired her. Ruth volunteered as a Master Gardener with a local university. The program emphasized water conservation, using "zero-scape" native Colorado plants for decoration. Ruth spent her time trying to outwit the gophers or deer terrorizing her own garden. She worked hard, and admired a strong work ethic in others. I smiled at her as we watched Kyle land the plane.

Kyle finished his flight and walked across the tarmac. He had stars in his eyes.

So, he began studying the ground school course for beginner pilots. Once he mastered the book work, he began flying once a week at a small airfield. He got so good, that he finally made his night flight and his cross country flight.

We had to have a physical for him by an F.A.A certified physician. After examining Kyle, this wonderful doctor mentioned that he had several amputees who were meeting with the F.A.A for flight certification. Kyle would eventually have to meet with them in Denver, when his hours and course work were complete. He needed the F.A.A okay before his first solo flight.

Mom called us a few weeks later.

She had been hiking with her hiking group that morning. She had related how frustrating it was for Kyle to find a job, even volunteering, despite the fact that he was second in his graduating class. The woman she was talking to, named Jeanne, related the story to her husband that night. Dave was a retired airline pilot who ran a home based business, refurbishing vintage aircraft. Jeanne called Mom the next day. She said that Dave had been up all night wrestling with wanting to help Kyle, after hearing his story. She said that Dave wanted to meet Kyle.

I was excited, as I told Rick about Dave and the Airplane community in Elbert. Dave, and several others lived, in houses on an airstrip. They flew their planes, and most of the houses had hangers instead of garages–or both. Some, like Dave, had several airplanes that they were rebuilding. Some of the planes were built from bare frames or a single engine.

We were mesmerized as we toured Dave's hanger, several weeks later. We made our introductions. Jeanne was so warm and welcoming. Dave took Kyle aside and introduced him to several of the other retirees. Some of the men were mechanics, some had worked for the FAA or the airlines. Jaime would be the mechanic that Kyle would volunteer under in order to gain experience. This would be very helpful, since most of the employers wanted a minimum of 2 year's experience working in the field. This had been the wall Kyle had run up against–employers wanted experience but how to get it when no one would hire you with out it? Volunteering would be the answer.

Kyle was so excited to learn about working on Vintage aircraft. He began to work with Jamie.

He came home exhausted on the days that he worked. He volunteered on the weekends, and was thrilled about all the things he was learning. He would relate the day's events excitedly, describing his day at dinner.

Kyle continued to look for work during the week. We felt helpless, because everything was computerized now. Rick and I felt like dinosaurs.

This went on for about a year. We were so thankful to Jeanne and Dave for encouraging Kyle–and to Jaime for working with Kyle, as well as supervising his work.

One step leads to another step. When we're fortunate, we meet kind people along the way who help us on our journey, or walk with us for a short time. The kindness that Kyle received from those compassionate people at Elbert was a blessing so profound, we felt in awe of what seemed like an invisible force guiding Kyle.

Kyle became stronger every day, and more confident in his work.

CHAPTER 16

Kyle Hired by Boeing, Despite Doctors' Discrimination

The phone rang one day.

"KYLE, IT'S FOR YOU!" I yelled downstairs.

Kyle listened. He got a pen and paper. He took some notes. He hung up the phone. He looked surprised.

"What? What?" I asked.

"Mom, that phone call was a Rep from Boeing. They want to interview me on the phone next week," Kyle said as he looked out the window in shock.

"Where?" I asked equally shocked as I sat down.

"Seattle," Kyle said softly trying to take it all in.

"Oh, my God," I whispered. I was thinking about the dream Kyle had had years ago which started all of this.

"Well, Kyle, you'll love the weather. It's by the Ocean. It rains everyday from Oct to April. The summers are beautiful there," I rambled absentmindedly.

I was screaming inside, "Oh My God! Seattle is so far away!"

I kept telling myself that we would be grateful for any job that Kyle could get as his first job after graduation. I took a deep breath and sighed. I thought back over the past year and wondered if God intended for Kyle to be patient, so that he might appreciate this opportunity more. I wondered if Kyle would appreciate the job more, too, and work harder to keep it. I thought all these things as I watched him prepare for his telephonic interview.

The day came, and Kyle sequestered himself downstairs to avoid distractions. Rick and I waited anxiously for the news. Kyle felt he had done well and had only struggled on a couple of questions.

"Mom, Redstone College really prepared me. I knew most of those questions. I think I really nailed it." Kyle seemed pleased with himself and hopeful.

We waited. Weeks passed.

Kyle got the call. The Boeing Company wanted him to fly up to Seattle, Washington for a second interview.

We celebrated that night, and I made one of Kyle's favorite dishes–Mediterranean rice with raisins and nuts, paired with garlic fish.

"Hey! Stop bitch slapping me with your stub," Caitlin snarled as Kyle was patting her shoulder with his stub.

"Stubbs RULE!" Kyle laughed with a sly grin.

"Are you nervous about going up there?" Rick questioned.

"Maybe you should go up with him, Rick." I muttered under my breath.

"Mom, I can handle it. I'm going to be okay," Kyle reassured me.

We grilled Kyle over the next few weeks. What to do in case of an emergency and who to call. We practiced going over interview questions and points to emphasize.

"Kyle repeat after me," Rick would say over and over. "I'm the guy who will come in early, and I'm the guy who will stay when everyone else goes home. I'm going to work harder than the other guy, and I'll be more grateful for the job, because I've worked so hard to achieve it."

We practiced possible situations and questions day after day.

The company had a wonderful system in place where the candidates were picked up at the airport and then taken to a hotel. Kyle was driven to the interview the next day, and given a tour of the different facilities.

There was some confusion over meeting places, so we guided Kyle over the phone on how to call people for answers.

I was so nervous watching him board that plane, but also I felt resigned. I knew that if he didn't go by himself, he wouldn't be able to inspire confidence in his fellow workers/ employers that he could do the job.

I had to let him go. It was the hardest thing I ever had to do.

And, I had to do it with a smile to show Kyle that I believed in him.

He called the next day.

"Well, Kyle, how do you think you did?" we asked together on the phone.

"I think I did pretty well. I messed up over two questions, but I knew everything else," Kyle responded.

"Did you get a chance to tell them you'd be a good worker?" Rick questioned.

"Yep, but mostly they wanted to know about my education from Redstone College."

"Wow, so what do you think?" I asked biting my lip nervously.

"I think I did pretty well!" Kyle said.

"You sound tired, Bud," Rick laughed.

"I am, I'll take it easy and see you tomorrow night," Kyle yawned.

We picked him up the next day at the airport. He related all the things he had seen. How much he liked the weather, which was rainy and foggy.

"Honestly, I just love the rain," Kyle said while hugging me.

"Seattle–it never occurred to me that you'd be going to Seattle," I mused.

"Well, we'll see!" Kyle sighed.

Kyle said he had gotten a good feeling from the people who worked there, and felt he had done a good job when the interviewers started joking around.

"Did they ask about the arm?" I asked.

"No. They said that they weren't allowed to ask, by law," Kyle said.

We waited.

Kyle was preparing for his first cross country flight while he waited for news from the company.

He was really excited.

"Remember to take extra money with you, Kyle, just in case!" Rick encouraged him.

Kyle was busy making his charts. Rick and I went with him to the flight school just before his big day.

"Look, Mom. There are T shirts signed by the students, when they make their first solo flight." Kyle looked up at the wall with appreciation.

"Wow!" I said.

"Yep, that's going to be me very soon," Kyle said wistfully.

He went cross country and came home, literally, walking on air.

I could see him growing in confidence every day, with every accomplishment–cross country, night flying, and passing exams.

He said he thought being a pilot, working in Alaska or over the Great Lakes, would be the ultimate job.

"Maybe, someday," Kyle said to himself.

Boeing called few weeks later. Kyle had the job providing he could pass the background check and the physical–drug test, hearing test, eye exam.

He labored over the forms that needed to be filled out online.

We arranged to have all the testing done. The drug testing was very strict and had to be done within a certain time frame which, once started, could not be postponed.

He completed all the forms and submitted them.

We waited.

Weeks went by and we waited.

We were beginning to get nervous.

The phone finally rang.

It was a nurse who was resubmitting some of the paperwork. She directed Kyle to get a note from his specialist, Dr Wilkins, to verify that he could do the work with his prosthetic.

We called Dr Wilkins' office and made arrangements to drive to Denver and get the exam and necessary paperwork. Dr. Wilkins was encouraging and extremely helpful.

We waited.

We played telephone tag with Boeing's Medical watch dog department.

We waited.

One day, a nurse from the company called. She told Kyle that she had a very difficult time believing that he could lift the required 70 pounds needed to comply with the job description. She was sending Kyle's file to the overseeing Doctor for review. The phone was on speaker. I couldn't believe my ears.

Kyle's face flushed red with fear and anger.

"Dr. Wilkins has assured you that I can do the job. I had my prosthetic custom made to withstand 75 pounds of pressure, and I have special attachments to do certain jobs like riveting or beveling," Kyle countered.

"Well, I'm sending this on to the company doctor. He'll get back to you after his review," she sniped.

I was fuming!

There was a deadline for the review to be completed. I felt like Kyle was being stonewalled by small minded, petty people.

The company doctor called some weeks later. He "clearly" did not believe that Kyle could do the physical work, regarding the 70 pound lifting. He said that Kyle was" clearly" disabled.

Kyle explained to him that he didn't think of himself as disabled, and hadn't applied as a disabled person. He could do the work.

We continued to play telephone tag with this medical department as the reviews continued. More forms needed to be completed.

Another nurse called and I answered. She said that she was reviewing the paperwork.

"I've been going over this application and I have a hard time believing that Kyle can do this work," she said with a sneer that turned into a "huff".

"His doctors who have seen and EXAMINED him have assured me that he can do the work. This information is already on file. You already have the name and number of the specialist to verify this," I said steadily to control my rising anger.

"Well, the company doctor will have to verify all of this, and he won't be back for a few days," she countered dismissively.

A week would go by and another nurse would answer the phone. I would be told that he didn't have any information, or would leave a message for another nurse.

I became angrier and more determined as the weeks passed.

Kyle became more discouraged.

I had had enough and said so to Rick.

"I've had it with these people. This is clearly prejudicial. They haven't examined Kyle, but they won't take Kyle's doctor's examination results. This is a clear violation of the Americans with Disabilities Act. Rick, if they find against him, it could ruin his chances of getting another job. One of the questions on job application forms is HAVE YOU EVER BEEN TURNED DOWN FOR A JOB? We can't allow this. We'll have to sue–sue them to overturn their arbitrary findings, or he'll suffer for this in the future. The irony of all this is that he doesn't want to be considered disabled, but it's the only law on the books that will protect someone like him."

"SUE BOEING!" Rick countered as if I had lost my mind.

"NO, BOEING IS A GREAT COMPANY. They gave Kyle the job. I'm going to sue that nurse and that doctor. They're denying him, based on their own prejudice, not on actual facts or an actual exam. Remember, he said, 'I'M not convinced that YOU can do it.' We'll sue the doctor and the petty nurse who started this whole thing. We'll have no choice if we want to save his future career. And, we'll sue them for the career Kyle would have had with the company. It could be millions over a 30 year life span. But, we'll probably end up broke in order to do it, unless we can find an attorney to work pro bono, or for free, until we get a monetary judgment."

Rick just shook his head. We were dreading the possibility of an upcoming battle. It was all so unnecessary, and worse, it was cruel.

My anger grew by the day. The weeks passed. Here was a kid that wanted to work. He wasn't asking for any handouts, he didn't feel a sense of entitlement because of his arm. He didn't use his disability to work the system or garner sympathy. He didn't think of himself as disabled, yet everyone else perceived him as "Unable". If we allowed these people to label him, no future employer would hire him.

If we sued to fight it, no future employer would hire him. We were SCREWED!

And so I prayed, and I prayed, AND I PRAYED!

"God, he can't have come this far only to let the small minded, mean spiritedness of others keep him from following his dreams. This can't be it. Please, God, send someone, anyone, willing to believe in Kyle. He wants to work, Lord, Please."

Christmas was coming and Kyle was in a "funk". He watched Caitlin and me put up her winter scene, which was a very "Dickens" English style village.

I asked him if he liked it.

He nodded. He liked the houses.

Tia, Cat's best friend, came over and admired the Christmas decorations.

I absentmindedly mentioned that Kyle should date a girl just like Tia. She was kind, thoughtful, strong and beautiful. She had a quiet kind of grace that comes from a gentle intelligence.

They both looked uncomfortable, although Tia thanked me for wanting her to be part of the family. Cat started to laugh.

"We just want to see a lot of little Tias running around the house," Cat joked as she pushed against Tia's arm playfully. Tia laughed.

Later, Kyle said that he thought of Tia as a sister and already part of the family.

I smiled and apologized for making them both uncomfortable.

"I was just thinking out loud, Kyle. You've never needed my help getting dates. All your girl friends have been beautiful, Honey," I said, taking a taste of the dinner I was cooking. I frowned. It needed more spices.

I took Kyle to lunch the next day at the mall. We walked through the shops. We came to one store that sold village scenes. He liked the Halloween scene with the automated flying witch.

"Look, it's even got flying monkeys!" Kyle said with a laugh.

Then he shrugged.

"I'm just not that into Christmas like you and Cat. Every bad news I've ever gotten has always been at Christmas. I HATE CHRISTMAS!" he said bitterly.

I stopped in my tracks. I was completely dumbfounded. I looked at him in shock.

"Kyle, Honey. It's not what you get out of Christmas. You've got it backwards. It's what you BRING to Christmas that's important. You've got to make Christmas fun for YOU, whatever that looks like. More importantly, you have to make Christmas a joy for those people around you. You're going to have children some day; you have to make it fun for them. What are you going to do, be Scrooge? That would be no fun for little ones."

"Hmm, I could have a Zombie Christmas!" Kyle laughed. "Or, No, an Alien Christmas. That might be cool."

"Okay, wisenheimer. Just don't scare the little ones," I choked up my coffee. "I don't want to hear my grandkids say, NO DADDY, PLEASE DON'T BRING OUT THE ZOMBIES."

Kyle drank his coffee and smiled. Zombies and aliens were Kyle's favorite things.

I watched him and I thought, "Well, why not? Hmmm, maybe that wasn't such a bad idea after all."

I got the whole family in on the idea.

We would make Kyle a unique winter scene that was completely Kyle–zombies, werewolves, aliens, dragons and mechanical items.

Rick and I found a pub house at a thrift store, and I found an Amish stable, because those two things are related, right? I laughed out loud. I found an automated zombie drinking a beer, and a green alien holding a raygun. Rick found a Dodge Viper in miniature and a light house. Cat bought trees and a glass pond. I put gravestones and a gargoyle behind the pub. I placed a small Terminator by the pond and a dragon by the stable.

It was perfectly bizarre.

It was so Kyle.

I brought it home.

"Kyle, come help me put this together." I yelled downstairs.

"What's this?" Kyle said his eyes wide.

"It's your Winter Scene," I laughed as I unpacked all the houses. "Now, this is just a start. Every year, I'll buy you a house or lamp post to build your village, which is what most people do. Oh, and I'll get you a dinosaur next year or a troll. What do you think?"

He just shook his head and smiled.

He helped me put it all together with the lights under the fake snow. We turned it on.

"Wow!" I said admiring my handiwork.

"It's different!" Kyle smiled. "I like it."

"It's awesome, Dude!" Cat laughed.

This began our tradition of a slightly creepy Christmas.

"Honestly, I think that I'd like a zombie themed wedding," Kyle laughed one day.

"I am NOT dressing up like the living dead for your wedding, Kyle!" I rolled my eyes.

"No, No! I know! We should all go to Disney World and have a Halloween wedding for Kyle," said Caitlin between munches on her candy cane. "We could throw popcorn or Halloween candy at the bride and groom."

"Hilarious!" I mumbled sarcastically, even though I smiled. Halloween was my favorite holiday.

Christmas came and went. It was subdued as we waited for news from the Doctors at Boeing, and with every day, we felt a little more discouraged.

Kyle continued to take flying lessons. It was the one thing that gave him hope. He was working on something for his future. A mechanic, who was also a pilot, was much more marketable. He began preparing for his night flights. He continued to work on Vintage airplanes at Elbert.

The phone rang sometime after the holidays.

"Kyle, it's for you!" I yelled downstairs.

"I'll get it!" he yelled back.

I was busy cleaning the kitchen.

Kyle slowly walked up the stairs and came into the kitchen. He was blinking hard.

"What's wrong?" I stopped and held a cup in my hand, motionless while the water continued to run.

"I got the job." Kyle said softly in disbelief.

"What job?" I was confused.

"THE JOB! I GOT THE JOB WITH BOEING! I HAVE 6 WEEKS TO GET THERE," Kyle yelled excited.

"Six weeks? February. Wow, what happened?" I asked incredulous.

"One of the bosses called Medical and asked where I was. The doctor said he didn't think I could do the job, lifting 70 pounds. The boss said he didn't care–I was hired as a quality control specialist, inspecting other people's work. I didn't need to lift 70 pounds. He told the doctor that he wanted me NOW."

"Oh, my God," I thought. It was an answer to prayer. I had asked God for just one person to help Kyle. I closed my eyes and silently said, "Thank you, Thank you, Thank you."

I immediately started packing things that Kyle would need. We put most of it in the garage: kitchen supplies, towels, and bedding. We packed up his room.

"Mom, I don't need 5 comforters." Kyle shook his head holding one up in the air.

"What if you get cold, what if I come to visit and I get cold, what if the heat goes out or there's an electrical storm,"

246

I obsessed out loud.

"What if the sky falls, Mom?" Kyle laughed.

"Funny. That's very funny. Hey when did you read Chicken Little?" I asked surprised.

"I listen. I listen to your stories," Kyle said with a slight smile.

"Okay," I said, distractedly thinking that somehow these silly rags would keep him safe.

Boeing would move Kyle's belongings to Seattle. We gave Kyle our couch.

"Why the couch?" My husband scratched his head.

"Because, we need a place to sleep when we visit Seattle," I responded with a smile.

"Okay," he nodded. It was a sleeper couch.

I went on line and looked up several apartments. I made appointments to tour them.

We would stay in a hotel for a few days, while we decided on the apartments.

We agreed that I would stay on long enough to help get him settled in his new place. I would help him establish new doctors, dentists, bank accounts–but really make him do it this time.

I was so happy for Kyle, even though I found myself in tears thinking about how far Seattle was from Colorado.

I was brushing my hair when I thought to myself, "Wouldn't it be great, Lord, if Kyle could meet Temple Grandin some-day. What an inspiration she would be for him. Just to give him encouragement. He seems so overwhelmed and unsure of this move. Please help him."

I smiled absentmindedly and thanked God for all our good fortune. I asked him to bless our upcoming trip to Seattle.

CHAPTER 17

Kyle Moves to Seattle, Washington

The day finally came. We decided to fly from Denver since we had the cat, Cynders, with us. Cat had to go to work early, and couldn't see us off. She was devastated. On the morning we were leaving to spend the night at Grandmas, there was a note on the fridge for Kyle. It was from Cat–her farewell letter.

It said, "Kyle, I know you will kick butt and take names in Seattle. I love you so much, and miss you already. Love Cat."

When Cat came home that night, we were already gone and staying with Rick's mother. Kyle had written her a reply.

"I love you so much and I will see you soon. Take care. Love Kyle." This little note was a lot from Kyle. Cat treasured it and cried, knowing he was leaving to start his new life.

We had spent the night at Grandma's and said our goodbyes early. She wished Kyle well.

"Hey, you're going to do great, Kyle!" Ruth said as we piled into the car.

The day was beautiful and sunny. Cynders wailed in the back seat. She finally calmed down. We sipped coffee and thoughtfully watched the scenery. Colorado is especially beautiful in the early morning, as the sun hits the snow capped Rocky Mountain peaks.

I sighed and recalled all the struggles that had brought us to this point.

We finally arrived at Denver International Airport. The parking lot was a huge sprawling complex.

Rick meandered over finding a parking space...and meandered, and meandered.

I became annoyed and looked at him thinking, "PICK A SPOT, ALREADY. IT'S JUST A PARKING PLACE. WHAT IS WRONG WITH YOU?"

"This looks good," he mumbled absentmindedly.

I looked at him like he had lost his mind, and I shook my head.

We got the cat and our luggage.

We walked to the nearest bus stop.

I looked up and saw a woman approaching the bus stop.

I blinked and looked again.

"Oh, my God, you're TEMPLE GRANDIN!" I said absolutely shocked.

She seemed surprised and opened her eyes, "Yes, I am."

"Oh my God, I'm so happy to meet you. I feel so blessed. This is my son Kyle. He has Autism too. He's just gotten a new job working with Boeing in Seattle," I rambled, pointing to my son.

"Well, don't tell me he's Autistic–tell me what he's doing," she said.

Kyle explained that he was an airplane mechanic and then he raised his arm.

"I just can't stand how some people have a sense of entitlement when they're disabled," she said.

I nodded, "I agree with you."

"Oh, you have a prosthetic. How does that work with being

a mechanic?" she asked somewhat surprised.

They walked on ahead talking, and she was pointing to his arm while nodding.

I was dumbfounded as I watched. It all seemed so surreal. We got off the bus and we became confused.

"Oh, it's this way. Just follow me! I do this all the time," Temple said.

Again, I blinked and shook my head.

Temple Grandin is leading the way, literally. What is wrong with this picture? I felt humbled in the weirdest way imaginable.

We thanked her as we got off the elevator. She wished Kyle good luck on his new job.

As I watched her walk away and shook my head again in amazement.

"Kyle, don't you feel blessed to have met Temple Grandin? Don't you feel encouraged starting your new life?" I said smiling. I was basking in this miracle.

Kyle turned around and looked at me quizzically.

"Mom, I got the impression that Temple Grandin needed to meet ME. Whenever you think you have it rough, there's always someone who has it a little rougher than you do," he replied, pointing to his prosthetic.

Kyle raised his arm. "She seemed really interested in how I was able to use my arm."

It never occurred to me that Kyle might be a blessing for Temple.

I felt profoundly moved by the whole experience, and, not a little, "like the joke was on me."

So, naturally, I told everyone I knew like a star struck teeny bopper. "Guess, Guess who I met..." I called all my cousins.

Yes, I'll never be one of those jaded Hollywood types that yawn, meeting new celebrities. No, I'm like a little kid who runs excitedly around, while dancing a little dance.

"You'll have to put that in your book!" my cousin Tina laughed.

My Book–it's been the family joke for years. I've been writing Poetry and Science Fiction for almost 20 years. So, it's a RUNNING joke, and we all laugh.

"Put this in your book," we all chime.

"I will definitely put this in my book," I laughed as we got to Airport Security.

We got in line and pulled out the cat. She was screaming a silent, terrified scream as she looked around at all the people. Her claws dug into my shoulder.

Kyle was up ahead and Security pulled him aside. They searched him, and then took him to a small room to the side.

We were asked to hold the cat while the carrier went through the x-ray machine.

Now, the cat was heavily drugged. We thought that was best. Imagine this cat, holding on for dear life, when I handed her to my husband's shoulder, her mouth still hanging open in that silent scream while looking around.

I knew exactly how she felt.

We proceeded to the room where Kyle was sitting. We peered into the room and saw that Kyle was hooked up to his own x-ray machine. They were examining the arm, with him still attached to it.

"What?" I thought as I watched the scene unfold. "Unbelievable!"

"They have to check for drugs and weapons," my husband

shrugged.

I watched. Kyle and the T.S.A security guard were laughing.

"See, he doesn't look any worse for wear," my husband smiled.

"Yeah, it's like my cousin Susan, who carries her Bible with her everywhere, as well as her breathing machine. She wears long skirts and sensible shoes. She's always searched at the airport," I laughed patting Rick's arm.

"Now, SHE looks like a Terrorist," He muttered sarcastically.

Kyle was finally released and we boarded the plane.

We arrived in Seattle a few hours later.

We picked up our rental car and drove to the hotel in Bellevue.

I had forgotten how lush and pretty Seattle was, even in February. It was rainy and foggy as we made our way to our room.

We let the cat out and she immediately ran around the room unsteadily, like a drunken sailor, tried to jump up on the counter and missed. She was glad to be out of her cage despite this.

We settled in, exhausted, and ordered Chinese food while we curled up and watched the Seattle news. Kyle's car was delivered the next day by the movers.

The next morning, we hooked up our GPS. It's a little machine that tells you how to find addresses. We plugged it in to find the apartments we had scheduled to visit.

We hadn't updated the GPS.

This was a mistake. The GPS told us to turn left into a lake and had us arrive "at destination" down a blind alley. When we turned into oncoming traffic, at the GPS' instruction, we realized our mistake. After the screaming stopped and we narrowly swerved to make a 360 turn, with cars passing us on all sides, we agreed.

UPDATE THE GPS!

We finally found the first place. The building was beautiful, just like the picture on the internet. It was also in the heart of the Ghetto–pawn shops, strip clubs, barred windows.

Kyle's eyes widened.

"Keep moving, Rick. I wouldn't put a dog in this neighborhood," I mumbled, as I bit my cheek.

Kyle was visibly relieved.

"Jesus!" Rick shrugged his shoulders in disgust.

We passed by several on the list, and finally came to the second appointment on our list.

The area still looked like city Ghetto to me, as I remembered my childhood in the Ghettos of Detroit. The mall was within walking distance, though, and there were lots of shops, as well as restaurants. The location was only 10 minutes away from Boeing.

We walked into the Apartment Manager's office and she seemed friendly. We toured the 2 bedroom apartment off the parking lot. Then we toured the 1 bedroom.

My heart skipped a beat when I saw the view.

Here in the middle of the industrial area, there was a green belt that gave the illusion of being in the forest–moss covered trees, wooded pathway with squirrels, birds flying everywhere. It was beautiful.

I knew this was the place for Kyle. It would be so serene to look out at that view.

We rented the apartment that day. We bought cleaning supplies as well as groceries.

We moved in the next day. The cat was extremely annoyed and commandeered the top of the refrigerator. She growled at us menacingly, so we left her alone while we blew up make shift beds.

We sat on the floor, eating pizza, and planned the next few days.

We went to banks and set up accounts the next day. We set up appointments for phone and television service. We were told that, under the "Anti Terrorism" laws, Kyle would have to go to the utility company in person, since he had no credit history.

By the time we were finished, Kyle had spent well over $2,000.00 in security deposits, due to his "lack of credit".

"Honestly, how does anyone do this without their parent's help, Rick?" I asked exasperated.

"I don't know. What DO people do without this kind of money?" Rick countered.

I fumed, thinking about all those poor kids, just starting out and getting "gouged" financially, under the guise of "no credit history".

Kyle set up most of the accounts himself. This was a shock, since everything was now online in this or that folder, with multiple pass words. He was a computer whiz.

This was beyond me.

The furniture arrived. Everything was in good shape except the pullout couch. It was completely broken.

Rick and Kyle worked on it and fixed it, but it was never the same. The head curved down at an angle just enough to make you feel like you were falling out of the bed. It was annoying, and it took forever to fall asleep at this odd angle.

Rick finally had to leave us and return to work. We drove

him down to the airport and dropped off the rental car.

He hugged us both.

"I'll see you in a month," I laughed.

"A MONTH?" he said shocked.

"I have a feeling it will be around the first of April. It's just radar," I shrugged.

Rick nodded knowingly, gave me a quizzical look and headed for security.

Kyle and I went back to the apartment. We spent the next week decorating his place. We put 2 comfortable chairs, facing the woods, where the dining table would have been. The dining room and kitchen had an Asian feel from the Japanese and Korean art on the walls. The bedroom was black and red with a huge Chinese embroidered Dragon over his bed. The bathroom was green and blue with pictures of F4 Phantom Jets that featured his father and grandfather in the cockpits. We found a place of honor for my dad's old police badges that Kyle admired. The living room was decorated with all the old Coats of Arms from our families–German knights, Irish knights, although I'm sure a horse thief was in there somewhere. Rick had engraved an old Roman style sword with the words: "Sir Knight of Flight". It was a special gift that Rick had given him the Christmas before the move.

Kyle admired the wall and the sense of history.

We finished hanging all the pictures of the family in the kitchen, so he would see our smiling faces at the beginning and end of each day. I thought it would make him feel less lonely.

I insisted that we buy some plants, which I told him would be good "oxygen" providers. I also bought him one beautiful orchid.

"Oh Mom, look how expensive it is," Kyle protested.

"It's beautiful, and it's your favorite flower." I waved my hand. "It's good for the soul, and I want you to have it."

We arranged them around the room and I breathed in the Asian spice mix of cloves, sandalwood and musk.

"Beautiful!" I smiled pleased with the results.

CHAPTER 18

Boeing, Seattle and a Cat Named Cynders

I spent the next few weeks making the last of the appointments to see the prosthetic company in Seattle.

It rained everyday–it rained and rained.

Kyle needed a new part for his arm, and I was frustrated. I was also a little scared.

"Of all the times for his arm to need repair, his probation was not one of the greatest," I thought.

We were fortunate to order the part, and Kyle could still use his spare arm.

I spent my afternoons cooking and reading while Kyle began his training.

He had the evening shift, so he arrived home late at night.

Did I mention it rained everyday?

I entertained the cat and put bird seed out for the birds. It became TV for the cat, and she watched the birds for hours. I put some milk out for a stray cat, only to find, to my dismay, that the cat began attacking Cynders through the window. I only had to say the word "Cat" and Cynders would come running, to look warily behind the window. I spent most of my time reading and dreaming for Kyle.

When he came home in the evenings, he came home soaked, and we would talk about his day. I would talk about the new mold that I had assassinated in the windows or on the door jams.

Seattle doesn't have the polite, pink mold that warns you, "I'm coming." NO–you look down one day and see the black mold spreading on windows and doors. It's not for the faint of heart.

The sun began to shine for several hours of the day later in March. The humming birds came and the view was magical. Rainbows were a common sight through the rain drops. I was convinced that this was the perfect temporary place for Kyle, until the sun went down.

That night, I heard a noise. I looked out the window.

"Oh, my God, You have RATS! Look, Kyle," I said horrified. I broke out into a cold sweat remembering the big black rats I saw as a child in Detroit.

"No, Mom. I think that's a possum. He's eating the breadcrumbs you left for the birds," Kyle laughed.

"Oh, you're right. It is a possum," I said, relieved, until it came up to the window and sniffed through the glass, baring its pointed teeth.

I continued to help Kyle with last minute touches to the apartment. I spent my time cooking, and finally took a much needed rest. I began reading some books that I had found at a used book store, and I enjoyed talking to Kyle about his days. We would talk about his impressions of the people who worked with him and his new boss. He was very happy to have a boss who appreciated him and his work.

I told Kyle that I felt I would be leaving the first week of April, but I was waiting to make sure that he had his health care in place. I would leave when he was completely covered under his new health care plan, and no longer needed me there for the transition.

I was stalling. I dreaded the day that I would have to leave him. I would joke about it, as a way of mentally preparing myself for the upcoming departure.

One night I looked at him and said he was ready for me to leave.

"I know I have to go, or I'll never have grandchildren, and I REALLY WANT GRANDCHILDREN. Okay, maybe not NOW, right this second, but I would like you to find a nice girl and settle down. You really can't do that with "MOM" hanging around your apartment," I grinned.

"Yeah, that would be creepy," Kyle laughed.

We prepared ourselves for the coming goodbye.

CHAPTER 19

Kyle Encourages a Parent Who Has an Autistic Child

April 1st came and Kyle finally received his health care. It was time for me to go home.

Kyle drove me to the airport and insisted on buying me a cup of coffee. We parted awkwardly, as I tried not to cry. I hurriedly drank my coffee. I hate long goodbyes, and I've never been able to languish over them. I feel a restlessness to get on with it when it's time to go.

Kyle's eyes brimmed with tears, but he looked away and gave me a quick hug.

I waved one last time, after going through security. I made it to my seat on the plane and then burst into tears.

Once the tears started, I couldn't stop.

I kept seeing him as a baby, walking that wooden duck along the living room floor. How could I leave my baby alone, so far away?

Oh, logically, I knew he was 22, but my mind kept seeing Kyle as that baby, and my heart responded.

I cry, even now, as I write these words.

The man sitting next to me asked me if I was alright.

My response went something like this:

"My baby… (cry, cry, cry)…Leaving my baby… (cry, cry, cry)…New job, (cry, cry, cry)…All alone, not ready… (cry,

cry, cry), " I sobbed.

He looked alarmed.

"Oh, Honey. It's okay. They grow up don't they?" he nodded sympathetically while patting my arm. "I'm moving my son to Colorado to go to college."

I nodded through my tears.

I came home and cried for a week. I missed Kyle so much. The months passed and summer finally came to the Rockies. One day Kyle called me.

"Hey, Mom! I had an interesting experience!" Kyle said excitedly.

"Yeah?" I waited.

"My boss came up to me the other day and asked me if I had ADHD–you know, because I don't sit still. Well, I told him, 'No, I have Autism, the high kind'." Kyle related.

"You have the high functioning kind!" I chimed.

"Yeah, and he was quiet for a moment. Then he said that I gave him hope. Apparently, his son is Autistic, and is 8 years old," Kyle said.

"Wow, what did you tell him?" I asked.

"I told him about the fish oil, and I told him to find something that his son is really passionate about. And I told him 'don't give up on your son'. My parents never gave up on me," Kyle paused.

I sat there stunned.

I had always hoped that Kyle would inspire others. I told him that he needed to inspire others in order to give back; otherwise, what was the point of all his struggles and his pain? What other purpose could there be than to make someone else's journey easier to bear, by giving them hope? And that's all any of us can do: tell our story and give some meaning to it, by allowing what we learned to help others.

At that moment, I felt profoundly awed by my son and the journey we shared together.

"Oh, and guess what?" he said excitedly.

"What?" I asked surprised.

"My Orchid is blooming!" Kyle shouted.

"Oh wow, that's wonderful Kyle," I laughed at his joy.

"Yep, yep, life is pretty sweeeeet," Kyle laughed.

"I'm happy for you, Kyle!" And I thought... "I'm so grateful for you."

"I'm happy for me too, Mom. Well, see you," Kyle hung up the phone.

I sat there for a moment.

The tears began to stream down my face, and I smiled.

The Orchid was Blooming!

CHAPTER 20

Epilogue - How Kyle Learned to Succeed

My son has since talked with many people. All of them had wished that they knew of someone who had Autism and had "MADE IT". Someone who could give them hope that their child would be okay. They're always surprised when Kyle tells them he is Autistic.

I have been amazed at how articulate Kyle has become, telling them how to help their Autistic children. While every child's Autism is different, Kyle usually emphasizes the things that helped him:

 * A high protein diet, emphasizing fish with vegetables– limit the fruits and carbs to evenings. A typical breakfast for Kyle is a can of fish and a handful of almonds or walnuts. Sometimes he'll have scrambled eggs with mushrooms and turkey bacon. Lunch is grilled chicken, turkey or some other low fat meat and vegetables. He drinks milk and low sugar V-8 juice (for his fruit), later in the day. Dinner is usually the meal when he'll have his carbohydrates–whole wheat toast, crackers, pasta, cereal, or rice dishes.

 * Fish oil helped Kyle. It helped Kyle focus and concentrate. No, he's not a doctor, and no, we don't know why. It just DOES. Maybe it will help your family. Legally, I'm sure I should put a disclosure in here somewhere–so....

check with your doctor. My thinking is that it's like Chicken Soup, "It couldn't hurt."

* Get them involved in some kind of community activity. Kyle's dancing lessons brought him out of his shell. Get them involved in some kind of physical activity that they can do to feel connected to a group–soccer, dancing, track and field, etc.–activities where the pressure is "off" to socialize verbally. Movement is the KEY to helping them learn and feel connected to their surroundings.

* Use the computer! It's very helpful, because the moving screen captures their attention and helps them hyper-focus.

* Find their passion and help them take the steps to accomplish their goals. Plan ahead, because you will be helping them with their lifetime goals also. It's okay to hold their hand while they do this. Who decided that when a kid turns 18, they magically know what they need to do to accomplish their goals???

* Don't necessarily believe that an "expert" knows more than you do about your child. You spend everyday with your child. While most professionals are well meaning, most of them spend too little time with your child to be an expert on ANYTHING.

* NEVER, NEVER, EVER GIVE UP ON YOUR CHILD. Autistic kids can do so much more than we imagine. Don't underestimate, and don't allow others to underestimate, what they can potentially do. They can and will surprise you.

*Gentle, loving repetition is very helpful in teaching children with Autism. Thank God, I tend to be a parrot. I repeat myself constantly, much to the weariness of those around me. Gentle is the key word. Sudden, loud noises or harsh reprimands will cause an Autistic child (and I suspect other children as well) to shut down in fear.

* There is some literature to suggest that people with "Autism have a vitamin D deficiency, which may be why vaccinations have been studied in relation to Autism..." (The Encyclopedia of Medical Breakthroughs and Forbidden Treatments, Medical Research Associates, Seattle, Washington, Copyright: 2009. pg. 35-39). I found this interesting since I have, according to my primary care doctor, one of the lowest vitamin D levels he's ever seen in his career as a doctor. I'm on prescription levels of Vitamin D now. Vitamin D is necessary for the body's immune system to fight off any number of toxins, viruses and bacteria. I was diagnosed later in life. What if I had this deficiency while pregnant and never knew?

These vitamins, foods and activities that I've mentioned, have all been helpful to Kyle's functioning in the real world. Would I change Kyle? No! His struggles have made him the wonderful man he is today. I would give him every resource available, however, to succeed in the world around him with more ease.

No one knows what causes Autism. It could be environmental toxins, genetic pre-disposition, vitamin deficiency, vaccinations or antibiotics. It could be gluten intolerance or sensitivity. It could be a combination of all of the above. It could be pig's wings and fairy dust, who knows? I wrote this story chronologically, hoping that my story might provide some insight into the causes of Autism.

I'm not interested in legal finger pointing or posturing. I'm only interested in solutions. I would hold "harmless", legally, any corporations willing to help us in the research to find the cause of Autism, under the Good Samaritan laws we have in this country. The corporations who create vaccines and antibiotics provide a valuable service. No one wants to return to the days when we had no vaccines, and could only watch as our children died or became crippled by polio, for example. Until we learn the exact causes of Autism, we could proceed more cautiously. Why not test all children for vitamin deficiencies, or give vitamins with the shots? Why not make sure that children don't have compromised immune systems, due to colds, infections or other conditions before, giving them vaccines? I'm sure that most parents wouldn't mind spending a little more to have vaccinations given one at a time over a longer period, rather than a "cocktail" before attending schools.

I was relating all of this to my cousin, Susan, one day, while we were driving around Colorado seeing the sights. Susan is a public health nurse, and very practical in her approach. She's really more like my sister, and no one tells you the truth like family.

She looked at me in exasperation.

"Why do you write all that nonsense about Vampires, Werewolves and Witches?" she asked.

"What do you mean?" I frowned. "I'll have you know, I intend to be famous when I'm dead."

"You should write about Kyle. He is SUCH AN INSPIRATION!" she said throwing her hands up in the air.

"You think people would want to read this story?" I shook my head. The thought never occurred to me to write it.

"YES!!!!!!" Susan laughed in mock disgust. "What's wrong with you?"

And so, I began writing Kyle's story that very night and showed her the first page the following morning.

She said she got goose bumps reading it. This has always been my clue that my Guardian Angel is telling me to pay attention, or that I'm on the right track.

And so, the story goes......

D. Levy.

BIBLIOGRAPHY

The Encyclopedia of Medical Breakthroughs and Forbidden Treatments (Health Secrets and Little-Known Therapies for Specific Health Conditions from A-Z), Medical Research Associates, Seattle, WA, USA, Copyright 2005

ABOUT THE AUTHOR

D. Levy has a Master's Degree of Social Work and was a former Assistant Director/teacher of an International Kindergarten program. She is currently an Author /Illustrator and resides in Colorado.

D. Levy can be contacted at:
DLevywheretheorchidblooms@yahoo.com